SAVING GRACE

A GUIDE TO FINANCIAL WELL-BEING

Leader Guide

Abingdon Press™

Nashville

Saving Grace
A Guide to Financial Well-Being
Leader Guide

978-1-7910-0839-0

20 21 22 23 24 25 26 27 28 29—10 9 8 7 6 5 4 3 2 1
MANUFACTURED IN THE UNITED STATES OF AMERICA

Contents

To the Leader

There's no getting around it: Money is a big issue, one that affects most aspects of our lives. A lot of our waking hours are focused on making it, spending it, worrying about it, fighting over it, trying to protect it, and trying to manage it.

Scripture is filled with teachings on wealth and money, and yet so many Christians seem to struggle in this area. Money is a powerful thing. Some even say that money is more than just a neutral medium that can be used for good or for bad; they would argue that money has a spiritual force or power, and that power is reinforced by cultural myths that have become a powerful force in shaping the very materialistic culture in which we find ourselves.

Bottom line: We're all affected by the myths of our consumer culture as it relates to money, and in this study we will examine many of these myths and contrast them with the faithful way toward money and how we spend and interact with it. We want to follow God's heart in the issue of money in our lives, and so we will get very practical in how to do that, using tools and biblical principles and applying them to our everyday financial lives.

Although individuals are able do this study on their own, going through the workbook in a group setting provides support, accountability, and encouragement that many people will find extremely helpful, and can help them get on a path to a healthy understanding of their finances and more control over this aspect of their lives.

You are an integral part of this process! Thank you for your commitment to helping others find biblical freedom over their finances.

How This Study Works

The goal of this study is for members to become grounded in a biblical understanding of a proper relationship to money and for each of them to commit to and develop a biblically based Spending Plan for their households.

Content Overview

In this study, we will:

- Contrast what our consumer culture says about money with what the Bible says about money.
- Show members how to track their expenses and evaluate their income.
- Discuss giving and saving.
- Address members' debt.
- Walk members through creating a personal Spending Plan that will guide them in every aspect of their financial lives.
- Encourage them in ways to experience peace, joy, and freedom in their financial lives.

What You Will Need for Each Session

In addition to this Leader Guide, as you facilitate this study you will need the following:

- The *Saving Grace Participant Workbook*
- The *Saving Grace: DVD* and access to a television and a DVD player with working remotes or a computer or other equipment capable of streaming video. (If you prefer streaming video files, you may purchase them at Cokesbury.com or access the videos via subscription at AmplifyMedia.com through an individual or church membership.)
- A calculator, computer, smart phone, or other device on hand for making any quick calculations.

- *Optional*: a markerboard or large sheets of paper and markers for recording or displaying group members' ideas and thoughts, as needed

It's also recommended that participants have access to Bibles, pens/pencils, and paper for note-taking during each session. Plan to provide those supplies if needed.

To the Leader: *Online resources including the forms in the Participant Workbook are available for download at: https://www.abingdonpress.com/savinggrace or at AmplifyMedia.com by searching "Saving Grace."*

Preparing for Your Sessions

This study contains six (6) sessions. (You may choose to add an introductory seventh session. See "Before the First Session" on page 4 for more information.)

Each session explores a different aspect of our financial lives, identifies the pull of our consumer culture in that area, and explores how the faithful way toward financial well-being can guide our decisions. Sessions 2-5 will walk members through completing a section of their master Spending Plan, and the last session will guide members in adjusting that plan.

Participants should complete each session in their workbooks before you meet as a group. Many of the activities in the workbook take some time and/or personal reflection, and you will not have time within your session to complete these activities.

The six sessions each take approximately one hour, but you will probably want to plan on 90 minutes for each meeting so that you have a little extra time in case your discussion runs over. (It's always better to finish early rather than rush to cram it all in!)

Each session is structured into a 60-minute format:

- Beginning Your Time Together (5-10 minutes)
- Video Session and Discussion (30-35 minutes)
- Study and Discussion (15 minutes)
- Closing activity and prayer (5 minutes)

Before the First Session—A Little Homework

In order for group members to get the most out of this study, they will need to complete six forms that comprise the Pre-Work section of their *Saving Grace Participant Workbook* (found on pages 7–13 of the workbook; also found at abingdonpress.com/savinggrace. Some of the digital forms found there can also do the calculations for participants.

It is very important that members complete the pre-work forms prior to beginning the study since they will be using their pre-work information throughout the study to establish their personal Spending Plans.

The pre-work forms are as follows:

1. Goals to Achieve This Year
2. What I Owe / What I Own
3. Gift List
4. What I Spend
5. Money Motivation Quiz
6. Money Autobiography

Communicating with the Group Before Your First Session

At least two weeks before you plan to meet for your first session, communicate with group members about the pre-work they will need to complete before you begin meeting. You may want to do this via email, or you might want to schedule an introductory session for the group to gather. In either format, be sure that the members understand the pre-work instructions and where to find the forms, and ask if they have any questions about completing those.

Completing the forms may take several hours, so advise them to begin as soon as possible.

Note to Leader: *Assure members that their personal financial information will remain confidential throughout the study. No one else—including the leader—is required to see any of their financial information, and they are not asked to share anything about their personal finances unless they offer that information themselves.*

WORKSHEET #1: GOALS TO ACHIEVE THIS YEAR

Please allow adequate time to give serious consideration to your goals. Carefully considered, realistic goals that flow out of what's really important to you are powerful motivators. That motivation will be very helpful to you in following through on the steps necessary to achieve your goals and ultimately, financial freedom!

Overall Goal

State your overall goal in starting this course. What do you hope will happen as a result?

My Goal:

Specific Goals to Achieve

Following are some possible goals that can serve as "thought starters" for you. The important thing is that the goals you list are ones that are truly important to you. Be as specific as you can, using dates, amounts, etc.

Pay off debt: _____

Save for: _____
(major purchase, replacement items, college, retirement)

Increase my giving to: _____

Become more disciplined in: _____

Other: _____

Other: _____

Other: _____

WORKSHEET #2: WHAT I OWE / WHAT I OWN

What I Owe				What I Own (optional)	
I Owe (Liabilities)	Amount	Minimum Monthly Payments	Interest Percentage*	I Own (Assets)	Amount
Mortgage (current balance)				Checking Account	
Home Equity Loans				Savings Account	
Credit Cards				Other Savings	
				Insurance (cash value)	
				Retirement	
				Home (market value)	
				Auto (market value)	
Car Loans				Second Auto (market value)	
Education Loans					
Family/Friends				Money Owed to Me	
Other				Other	
				Other	
Total of All I Owe				Total of All I Own	

*Note: Enter percents as .03 for 3%, .10 for 10%, etc.

Net Worth (optional)

Total of All I Own – Total of All I Owe = Net Worth (in earthly terms, not God's!)*

$ _____ – $ _____ = $ _____

*Never confuse your self-worth with your net worth. In God's eyes each one of us is of infinite worth.

WORKSHEET #3: GIFT LIST

List the names of those for whom you buy gifts and the amounts you typically spend on each occasion.*

Name	Birthday	Christmas	Anniversary	Other
1.				
2.				
3.				
4.				
5.				
6.				
7.				
8.				
9.				
10.				
11.				
12.				
13.				
14.				
15.				
16.				
17.				
18.				
19.				
20.				
Total				

Grand Total (of all columns) $ _____

Monthly Average (Total ÷ 12) = $ _____

*You may wish to also include the cost of holiday decorations, entertaining, etc.

WORKSHEET #4: WHAT I SPEND

What I Spend

Earnings/Income Per Month	Totals
Salary #1 (net take-home)	_____
Salary #2 (net take-home)	_____
Other (less taxes)	_____
Total Monthly Income	$ _____

% Guide*

1. Giving $ _____

    Church   _____
    Other Contributions   _____

2. Savings   15% $ _____

    Emergency   _____
    Replacement   _____
    Long Term   _____

3. Debt   0-10% $ _____

    Credit Cards:
      Visa   _____
      MasterCard   _____
      Discover   _____
      American Express   _____
      Gas Cards   _____
      Department Stores   _____
    Education Loans   _____
    Other Loans:
      Bank Loans   _____
      Credit Union   _____
      Family/Friends   _____
      Other   _____

4. Housing   25-36% $ _____

    Mortgage/Taxes/Rent   _____
    Maintenance/Repairs   _____
    Utilities:
      Electric   _____
      Gas   _____
      Water   _____
      Trash and Recycling   _____
      Telephone/Internet   _____
      TV/Streaming Services   _____
      Other   _____

5. Auto/Transp.   15-20% $ _____

    Car Payments/License   _____
    Gas & Bus/Train/Parking   _____
    Oil/Lube/Maintenance   _____

6. Insurance   5% $ _____
    (Paid by you)

    Auto   _____
    Homeowners   _____
    Life   _____
    Medical/Dental   _____
    Other   _____

7. Household/Personal   15-25% $ _____

    Groceries   _____
    Clothes/Dry Cleaning   _____
    Gifts   _____
    Household Items   _____
    Personal:
      Tobacco & Alcohol   _____
      Cosmetics   _____
      Barber/Beauty   _____
    Other:
      Books/Magazines/Music   _____
      Allowances   _____
      Personal Technology   _____
      Extracurricular Activities   _____
      Education   _____
      Pets   _____
      Miscellaneous   _____

8. Entertainment   5-10% $ _____

    Going Out:
      Meals   _____
      Movies/Events   _____
      Babysitting   _____
    Travel (Vacation/Trips)   _____
    Other:
      Fitness/Sports   _____
      Hobbies   _____
      Media Subscriptions   _____
      Other   _____

9. Prof. Services   5-15% $ _____

    Child Care   _____
    Medical/Dental/Prescriptions   _____
    Other:
      Legal   _____
      Counseling   _____
      Professional Dues   _____

10. Misc. Small Cash   2-3% $ _____
     Expenditures

Total Expenses $ _____

* This is a percent of total monthly income. These are guidelines only and may be different for individual situations. However, there should be good rationale for a significant variance.

TOTAL MONTHLY INCOME	$ _____
LESS TOTAL EXPENSES	$ _____
INCOME OVER/(UNDER) EXPENSES	$ _____

WORKSHEET #5: MONEY MOTIVATION QUIZ

Directions

For each of the questions below, circle the letter that best describes your response. There are no right or wrong answers here, just more insight into why you see and interact with money the way that you do.

1. Money is important because it allows me to . . .
   a. Do what I want to do.
   b. Feel secure.
   c. Get ahead in life.
   d. Buy things for others.

2. I feel that money . . .
   a. Frees up my time.
   b. Can solve my problems.
   c. Is a means to an end.
   d. Helps make relationships smoother.

3. When it comes to saving money, I . . .
   a. Don't have a plan and rarely save.
   b. Have a plan and stick to it.
   c. Don't have a plan but manage to save anyway.
   d. Don't make enough money to save.

4. If someone asks about my personal finances, I . . .
   a. Feel defensive.
   b. Realize I need more education and information.
   c. Feel comfortable and competent.
   d. Would rather talk about something else.

5. When I make a major purchase, I . . .
   a. Go with what my intuition tells me.
   b. Research a great deal before buying.
   c. Feel I'm in charge—it's my/our money.
   d. Ask friends/family first.

6. If I have money left over at the end of the month, I . . .
   a. Go out and have a good time.
   b. Put the money into savings.
   c. Look for a good investment.
   d. Buy a gift for someone.

7. If I discover I paid more for something than a friend did, I . . .
   a. Couldn't care less.
   b. Feel it's OK because I also find bargains at times.
   c. Assume they spent more time shopping, and time is money.
   d. Feel upset and angry with myself.

8. When paying bills, I . . .
   a. Put it off and sometimes forget.
   b. Pay them when due, but no sooner.
   c. Pay when I get to it, but don't want to be hassled.
   d. Worry that my credit will suffer if I miss a payment.

9. When it comes to borrowing money, I . . .
   a. Simply won't/don't like to feel indebted.
   b. Only borrow as a last resort.
   c. Tend to borrow from banks or other business sources.
   d. Ask friends and family because they know I'll pay.

10. When eating out with friends, I prefer to . . .
    a. Divide the bill proportionately.
    b. Ask for separate checks.
    c. Charge the bill to my credit/debit card and have others pay me.
    d. Pay the entire bill because I like to treat my friends.

11. When it comes to tipping, I . . .
    a. Sometimes do and sometimes don't.
    b. Just call me Scrooge.
    c. Resent it, but always tip the right amount.
    d. Tip generously because I like to be well thought of.

12. If I suddenly came into a lot of money, I . . .
    a. Wouldn't have to work.
    b. Wouldn't have to worry about the future.
    c. Could really build up my business.
    d. Would spend a lot on family and friends and enjoy time with them more.

13. When indecisive about a purchase, I often tell myself . . .
    a. It's only money.
    b. It's a bargain.
    c. It's a good investment.
    d. He/she will love it.

14. In our family . . .
    a. I do/will handle all the money and pay all the bills.
    b. My partner does/will take care of the finances.
    c. I do/will pay my bills and my partner will do the same.
    d. We do/will sit down together to pay bills.

Score: Tally your answers by the number of times you chose each letter.

a. _____   c. _____
b. _____   d. _____

To understand your results, see the explanation on the back of this page.

UNDERSTANDING THE RESULTS OF YOUR MONEY MOTIVATION QUIZ

Money means different things to different people based on a variety of factors, such as temperament and life experiences. Often the meaning of money and the way it motivates us is subtle and something we are not always aware of. This simple quiz is designed to give you an indication of how strongly you are influenced by the following money motivations: Freedom, Security, Power, and Love.

The key to your money motivation is reflected in the relative number of A, B, C, or D answers.

"A" answers indicate that money relates to Freedom. To you, money means having the freedom to do what you like.

"B" answers indicate that money relates to Security. You need to feel safe and secure, and you desire the stability and protection that money supposedly provides.

"C" answers indicate that money relates to Power. Personal success and control are important to you, and you appreciate the power money sometimes provides.

"D" answers indicate that money relates to Love. You like to use money to express love and build relationships.

One of the keys to managing money wisely is to understand our relationship to it. We hope this exercise gives you some helpful insights. You may wish to share your scores with your spouse or a friend and discuss whether their perceptions of your money motivations are consistent with your scores.

WORKSHEET #6: MONEY AUTOBIOGRAPHY

Often how we relate to our money and possessions is heavily influenced, positively or negatively, by our early life experiences and how money was handled in the households we grew up in. Taking time to reflect upon the following questions can make us aware of those influences and allow us to take steps to change any negative behaviors they may have fostered.

Your History with Money

1. How would you describe your life with money so far?
2. How was money handled in your family? Who was your family's Chief Financial Officer?
3. Would you call your family of origin rich, poor, or neither?
4. What did you think about money as a child?
5. Did you have an allowance? How did that affect your relationship to money?
6. When you were growing up, did your family talk about money?
7. Would you call your family generous? If so, where did they give money?
8. What messages did you receive about giving and saving money?
9. How was money tied to faith in your family?

Money in Your Current Life

1. Who are your current financial role models?
2. In your current family, who handles the money?
3. If you have children, do you discuss money issues with them?
4. What are your practices of generosity? Do you tithe?
5. Do you feel that money is abundant or scarce?
6. Do you feel like you can afford what your family needs?
7. How much money comes through your life in a year? ten years?
8. How is your relationship with money related to your relationship with God?

Helpful Hints for Managing Your Sessions

Preparing for Each Session

- Pray for wisdom and discernment from the Holy Spirit, for you and for each member of the group, as you prepare for the study.

- Before each session, familiarize yourself with the content. Read through the workbook session again, and read through the session in this Leader Guide in its entirety.

- Make notes or mark the specific discussion questions you plan to cover during your session. Be prepared, however, to adjust the session as group members interact and as questions arise. Prepare carefully, but allow space for the Holy Spirit to move in and through the group members and through you as facilitator.

- Prepare the space where the group will meet so that the space will enhance the learning process. Ideally, group members should be seated around a table or in a circle so that all can see one another. Moveable chairs are best, so that the group easily can form pairs or small groups for discussion, if your group is large. You may want to serve water, coffee, or other refreshments to your members.

- Communicate with group members a few days before the session to let them know what you'll be covering this week.

Shaping the Learning Environment

- Create a climate of openness, encouraging group members to partici-pate as they feel comfortable.

- Remember that some people will jump right in with answers and comments, while others need time to process what is being discussed.

- If you notice that some group members seem never to be able to enter the conversation, ask them if they have thoughts to share.

Give everyone a chance to talk, but keep the conversation moving. Moderate to prevent a few individuals from doing all the talking.

- If no one answers at first during discussions, do not be afraid of silence. Count silently to ten, then say something such as, "Would anyone like to go first?" If no one responds, venture an answer yourself and ask for comments.

- Model openness as you share with the group. Group members will follow your example. If you limit your sharing to a surface level, others will follow suit.

- Encourage multiple answers or responses before moving on.

- Ask, "Why?" or "Why do you believe that?" or "Can you say more about that?" to help continue a discussion and give it greater depth.

- Affirm others' responses with comments such as "Great" or "Thanks" or "Good insight"—especially if it's the first time someone has spoken during the group session.

- Monitor your own contributions. If you are doing most of the talking, back off so that you do not train the group to listen rather than speak up.

- Remember that you do not have all the answers. Your job is to keep the discussion going and encourage participation.

Managing the Session

- Honor the time schedule. If a session is running longer than expected, get consensus from the group before continuing beyond the agreed-upon ending time.

- Involve group members in various aspects of the group session, such as saying prayers or reading Scripture.

- As always in discussions that may involve personal sharing, confidentiality is essential. Group members should never pass along stories that have been shared in the group. Remind the group members at each session: confidentiality is crucial to the success of this group.

Ending the Study

- Your members have worked very hard to complete this study. At end of your last session, consider having a party or celebration to celebrate what they have accomplished in creating and committing to their Spending Plans.

- Accountability and follow-up are important to reaching our goals. Consider setting a session four to six weeks out for the group for a check-in meeting, or commit to calling and following up with them individually at that time to see how participants are faring in their goals.

Tips for Online Meetings

Meeting online is a great option for a number of situations. During a time of a public-health hazard, such as the COVID-19 pandemic, online meetings are a welcome opportunity for folks to converse while seeing each other's faces. Online meetings can also expand the "neighborhood" of possible group members, because people can log in from just about anywhere in the world. This also gives those who do not have access to transportation or who prefer not to travel at certain times of day the chance to participate.

There are a number of platforms for online meetings. Google has two products, one called Google Hangouts and one called Google Meet. You need only a Google account to use them, and they are free.

Another popular option is Zoom. This platform is used quite a bit by businesses. If your church has an account, this can be a good medium. Individuals can obtain free accounts, but those offer meetings of no longer than forty (40) minutes. For longer meetings (which you will want for this study), you must pay for an account.

Some platforms to consider: GoToMeeting, Web Meeting, Microsoft Teams, and others. Search the internet for "web conferencing software," and you will probably find a link to top-ten rating sites that can help you choose.

Training and Practice

- Choose a platform and practice using it, so you are comfortable with it. Engage in a couple of practice runs with another person.
- Set up a training meeting.
- In advance, teach participants how to log in. Tell them that you will send them an invitation via email and that it will include a link for them to click at the time of the meeting.
- For those who do not have internet service, let them know they may telephone into the meeting. Provide them the number and let them know that there is usually a unique phone number for each meeting.
- During the training meeting, show them the basic tools available for them to use. They can learn others as they feel more confident. Make the meeting fun by showing some amusing content, such as the Facebook page Church Humor (www.facebook.com/ChurchLOL/).

During the Meetings

- **Early invitations.** Send out invitations at least a week in advance. Many meeting platforms enable you to do this through their software.
- **Early log in.** Participants should log in at least ten minutes in advance, to test their audio and their video connections.
- **Talking/not talking.** Instruct participants to keep their microphones muted during the meeting, so extraneous noise from their location does not interrupt the meeting. This includes chewing or yawning sounds, which can be embarrassing! When it is time for discussion, participants can unmute themselves. However, ask them to raise their hand or wave when they are ready to share, so you can call on them. Give folks a few minutes to speak up. They may not be used to conversing in web conferences.

All Manner of Good

Planning the Session

Session Goals

Through this session's discussion and activities, participants will be encouraged to:

- Think about their own tendencies toward money and possessions as idols;
- Learn what the faithful way has to say about money; and
- Realize the benefits of a Spending Plan and how it can help them faithfully achieve their financial goals.

Preparation

- Read and reflect on the Introduction and chapter 1 of *Saving Grace Participant Workbook*. This session should be conversational, warm, and inviting. It lays the foundation for what might be a new perspective on personal finances and, for many, will be the first time they are aware of the spiritual significance of their relationship to money.
- Read through this session outline in its entirety to familiarize yourself with the material being covered. Be prepared to adjust the session as group members interact and as questions arise. Prepare carefully, but allow space for the Holy Spirit to move in and through the group members and through you as facilitator.

- Read and reflect on the following key Scriptures:
- 1 Timothy 6:10
- Isaiah 55:2
- Matthew 6:24
- Hebrews 13:5
- You may want to have a markerboard or large sheet of paper available for recording group members' ideas.
- You will need access to a DVD player or another method for streaming videos online for the group to watch.
- Have a Bible, paper for taking notes, and a pen or pencil available for every participant.

Beginning Your Time Together (5-10 minutes)

As participants arrive, welcome them to this study. Depending on how familiar participants are with each other, you might want to spend a few minutes introducing yourselves and sharing why you are interested in doing this study. You might conclude by briefly sharing what has led you to be teaching this class, which could include key aspects of your own financial and faith journey.

Open the group in prayer; then ask the following icebreaker question and encourage participants to share their responses with the group.

Opening Prayer

Heavenly God, we are thankful for time to gather together and explore an area of our lives that is so meaningful, but can sometimes feel overwhelming. Help us to know that you are with us, and that you are guiding us as we seek to be financially faithful to you; in Jesus's name. Amen.

Icebreaker

- When you were a kid, what were your thoughts on money? For example, what did you think happened when your parents wrote a check or used a card to pay for something? What's your earliest "money" memory?

Video Session (30-35 minutes)

Watch video session (15-20 minutes in length).

Video Discussion

- What financial education did you receive as a child, a young adult, or an adult? Do you relate to Anna's story about her dad's basic advice to simply "spend less than you make"? Have you found that advice helpful, or not?

- Do you currently feel your money is a tool that works for you, or the other way around?

- Tom says that his wife's commitment to tithing early on in their marriage pushed him to consider the difference between what he needed and what he wanted, and that he realized he struggled with anger about not getting all the things he wanted. Do you relate to Tom's story? How do you think you are ruled by your needs and wants?

- As a young pastor, Anna found that, although Jesus talks a lot about money in the Bible, many members of her congregation were very uncomfortable talking about money and how it should be used. Have you found this to be true? Why do you think this is often the case?

- The Methodist tradition follows John Wesley's direction to "make all you can, save all you can, and give all you can." Wesley saw how money often corrupts, but also how money used well can be used to serve God's people now, here on earth. How have you seen money or resources put to use to serve God's purposes in this world?

- Tom and Anna talk about how a spending plan can be a spiritual discipline and not just a financial one because writing down how we spend our money reveals our priorities. What makes you nervous or hesitant about starting this process?

- When it comes to money, there are often generational differences in the ways that people choose to spend or save or give their money. What do you see people in your generation struggling with when it comes to money issues?

Study and Discussion (15 minutes)

Note to Leader: *Based on the interests of your group and the time allowed, use as many or as few of these discussion topics and prompts as you'd like.*

Ask for volunteers to look up and read aloud the following verses in the Bible that reference money.

- 1 Timothy 6:10 ("The love of money is the root of all kinds of evil.")
- Isaiah 55:2 ("Why spend money for what isn't food, / and your earnings for what doesn't satisfy?")
- Matthew 6:24 ([Jesus said,] "No one can serve two masters. Either you will hate the one and love the other, or you will be loyal to the one and have contempt for the other. You cannot serve God and wealth.")

Ask,

- How do these verses expose money's potential effects on the state of our hearts? How does it affect our thoughts and actions?
- In the Activity: The Idols We Keep (page 17 in the workbook), we acknowledged that though money itself is not innately a bad thing, it can become an idol—even a rival god—in some people's lives. Has there ever been a time in your life when you felt money became an idol in your life? How did it affect you?
- When have you been in a situation where you felt the tension in your heart between how to manage your money well and how to honor God? What happened?

What Our Consumer Culture Says About Money

- In the Activity: The Myths We Believe (found on page 18 of the workbook), we are given three myths our consumer culture feeds us on a regular basis:

  ◊ Things bring us happiness.

  ◊ Debt is expected and unavoidable.

  ◊ A little more money will solve all my problems.

- Which myth do you think influences you the most? How has believing this myth influenced the way you live your life?

Money and the Faithful Way

In Scripture, we see three core truths about how God tells us to use our resources:

1. God created everything. (Genesis 1)

2. God owns everything. ("The earth is the Lord's, and everything in it, / the world and its inhabitants too" [Psalm 24:1].)

3. We are trustees, not the owners, of all God has made. (First Corinthians 4:2 says, "In this kind of situation, what is expected of a manager is that they prove to be faithful.")

- When it comes time for you to use your money or other resources, do you typically think about any of these core truths? What usually dictates how you spend your money?

- In the Activity: Owner or Trustee? (found on page 20 of the workbook), you were asked to reflect on how you see yourself, whether as an owner or a trustee.

Note to Leader: *If you have a markerboard or large piece of paper available, you might want to draw the continuum graphic and ask participants to come up and place an X where they currently fall on the continuum.*

Reflect on your own finances and possessions. Put an X on the continuum below to reflect how you see yourself, whether as an owner or a trustee.

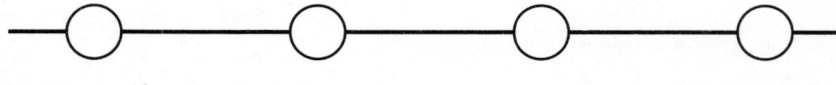

I see myself as
an owner

I see myself as
a trustee.

Repeat the activity while considering specific things: of my home, of my salary, of my time.

KEY QUESTION

Will God consider my financial decisions to be faithful or foolish?

- Would anyone be willing to share where he or she saw him- or herself on the continuum of owner or trustee?
- How does having the mindset that you are trustee of God's resources change the way you think about money in general?

The Pull of the Consumer Culture vs. the Faithful Way

FINANCIAL WELL-BEING

The contentment we feel as we faithfully manage our financial resources according to God's principles and purposes.

- Have you ever fallen into the "bigger barns" mindset? What was the situation, and how did it affect your life or finances?
- On page 22 of the workbook, you will see a list of five areas—earning, giving, saving, debt, and spending—we will cover as we discuss our financial lives. In which of the five financial areas do you feel you need to grow? How might growth in that area lead you to be a faithful trustee of God's resources?

Why Create a Spending Plan?

- What is your initial reaction to the word *budget*? What has been your past experience in working with or living on "a budget"?

- Currently, where do you stand with using or implementing a budget?

- In what areas do you tend to struggle the most to contain your spending?

> **THE SPENDING PLAN:**
>
> The fundamental tool that enables us to control our money so that it doesn't control us.

Closing Activity and Prayer (5 minutes)

Note to Leader: *As you close this week's session, plan to take a few minutes for participants to quietly reflect on what you have discussed during this session. If you sense your members are open to it, you may want to ask if anyone would like to share his or her answers afterward. An Action Plan for the Week follows, as well as a sample closing prayer.*

The hope of this study is for you to live in the freedom that comes from following God and using those resources entrusted to you to the best of your ability, and we know this plan can help you get there. We are all here to walk this path together and support each other along the way.

- What one word would you use to describe your relationship to your finances at this point? Take a moment to envision what word you hope will describe your finances at the end of this study. Write down that word somewhere in your workbook to remind you of your goal.

- As you read through chapter 1, what new insights did you gain into the role of money in our spiritual lives?

- What are some specific things you hope to accomplish through this study?

Action Plan for the Week

In our next session we will be referring to the "Goals to Achieve This Year" form from the pre-work. If you haven't already completed these forms, try to do so before our next meeting.

Closing Prayer

God, thank you for the opportunity to explore our finances in light of your desires for us and how you desire we live out truth in your name. We come to you humbly, asking you to guide us as we seek to be trustees of all you have entrusted to us. Give us the strength to dive deep into our hearts and our attitudes to discover those areas that cause us trouble. We bring our finances and leave them at your feet, Lord. Guide us and lead us to freedom in this area of our lives, and in the entirety of our lives; in Jesus's name. Amen.

Getting Started: Tracking Expenses and Income

Planning the Session

Session Goals

Through this session's discussion and activities, participants will be encouraged to:

- Set goals they want to achieve this year;
- Learn how to track their daily expenses; and
- Complete the Income section of their Spending Plans.

Preparation

- Read and reflect on chapter 2 of *Saving Grace Participant Workbook*.
- Read through this session outline in its entirety to familiarize yourself with the material being covered. Be prepared to adjust the session as group members interact and as questions arise. Prepare carefully, but allow space for the Holy Spirit to move in and through the group members and through you as facilitator.
- Read and reflect on the following Scriptures:
  ◊ 1 Timothy 6:10
  ◊ Ecclesiastes 9:10
  ◊ John 10:10

◊   Genesis 1:27

◊   Colossians 3:23

- You may want to have a markerboard or large sheet of paper available for recording participants' ideas or for putting your own thoughts on the board for the group to see.

- Have a Bible, paper for taking notes, and a pen or pencil available for every participant.

- You will also want to have a calculator, computer, smart phone, or other device on hand for making any quick calculations.

- You will need access to a DVD player or another method for streaming videos online for the group to watch.

- This week you'll be asking participants to refer back to the "Goals to Achieve This Year" form they completed in pre-work. If you'd like, send an email reminder a few days prior to your meeting time, reminding participants to make sure they complete this form before you meet.

Beginning Your Time Together (5-10 minutes)

As participants arrive, welcome them. If you've had any new members join the group this week, be sure to make introductions to the other members.

Open the group in prayer; then ask the following icebreaker question and encourage participants to share their responses with the group.

Opening Prayer

Dear God, thank you for time to gather together again this week. As we talk about our income and the importance of developing a Spending Plan, help us to know that our value is based solely on who you say we are, not on what is stated on our bank accounts. Turn our hearts toward you through our conversation today; in Jesus's name. Amen.

Icebreaker

- What are some ways the "pull of the consumer culture" regarding money or possessions impacted you this week?

Video Session (30-35 minutes)

Watch video session (15-20 minutes in length).

Video Discussion

- Cary points out that his mother would sometimes say, "I'd love to buy that for you, but it's not in the budget at this time." When there is something that you want or need, do you tend to spend that money without question, or are you able to pause and consider it further? What about if it's something someone in your family wants or needs?

- In the past, have you had goals that helped guide your finances? How did those goals affect your spending?

- Anna and Cary discuss how, as disciples, we need to have a good theology of money, though sometimes it's hard to discuss in church or small group settings because most of us think of money as our own and not something that should be incorporated into our discipleship journey. Have you ever thought about your own theology of money? How would you define it?

- What we spend our money on reflects what we value. Based on that statement, what would your current values be?

- Cary pointed out that a lot of people are hesitant to track their expenses because they want to avoid seeing the reality of their spending. Do you identify with this? Why or why not?

Study and Discussion (15 minutes)

Note to Leader: *Based on the interests of your group and the time allowed, use as many or as few of these discussion topics and prompts as you'd like.*

Ask,

- What are some of the lies you've always believed about money? What are some truths you've learned?

- In the past, have you been resistant or reluctant to take an honest look at your spending? If so, why do you think that is? In what ways might that reluctance be affecting your financial life?

- Does John Wesley's take on money (found on page 28 of the workbook) surprise you? If so, why?

- What do you consider "honest industry"? What are its benefits?

The Benefits of a Spending Plan

- A Spending Plan benefits everyone—at all points along the economic continuum—and not just for people in financial difficulty, as we often believe. A Spending Plan:

  ◊ Allows us to face reality.

  ◊ Avoids waste.

  ◊ Keeps our values and priorities in the forefront.

  ◊ Leads to financial freedom.

- Ask for a volunteer to read aloud John 10:10. ("I came so that they could have life—indeed, so that they could live life to the fullest.") How can thoughtfully, honestly, and prayerfully examining your financial life lead you to live life to the fullest?

- Explain this statement in your own words: "When our financial picture is mysterious, we aren't able to connect our finances with our faith in a clear way." Do you think that's true? In what ways?

- On page 30 of the workbook (Activity: Benefits of a Spending Plan), you were asked to put a check mark by the one benefit you think will most impact your life. Which benefit did you choose and why? What do you hope to gain in that area?

Your Goals

- On page 30 of the workbook, you were asked to revisit your "Goals to Achieve This Year" pre-work form and to see if any of those goals have changed since we started this course together. Invite participants to share by asking:

  ◊ Did any of your goals shift or change from your pre-work until now?

  ◊ Why do you think it's important to have goals for your financial life? How do goals help motivate you personally?

Track Your Expenses

- On pages 32–33 of the workbook, you see a form titled "Spending Record Example." After looking over this form and the explanation on pages 31 and 34 of the workbook, does anyone have questions about how the form is filled out?

- Was there anything that tripped you up on the Activity: Recording Receipts (on pages 36–37 of the workbook)? Did you learn anything new or helpful from that activity?

- Notice the Hints for Tracking Your Expenses sidebar (found on page 35 of the workbook). Did you learn any new tips from that information?

- Hopefully we've convinced you that keeping track of your expenses is something that is very doable and can help you really see what you're spending. On pages 34–36 of the workbook, three action steps are given for getting started on tracking your expenses:

  1. Save your receipts.

  2. Record your purchases every day.

  3. Create a miscellaneous Small Cash category.

- Are you already doing any of these three actions? If so, what is working for you, and what's not?

- In what areas do you have the most trouble keeping track of your expenses? Have you learned anything in this session that might help you?

- Does anyone want to share any other tips you have found helpful or essential for keeping track of expenses?

- The workbook asks a key question: "Is it worth two minutes a day of record keeping to bring this crucial area of my life—my spending—under control?" How do you respond to this question?

- On page 37 of the workbook (Activity: Which Form Will You Use?), you were asked to choose the method by which you will record your expenses for the next month. Which one did you choose? Why?

WHAT OUR CONSUMER CULTURE SAYS ABOUT **EARNING**

- Your value is measured by your position, your paycheck, the kind of car you drive, or the house you live in.
- A little more money will solve all your problems.

EARNING AND THE FAITHFUL WAY

- Our value is not measured by what we earn or do, but by who we are: beloved [children] of God, created in the image of God (Genesis 1:27).
- We are called to work with commitment, purpose, and a grateful attitude (Colossians 3:23).

Track Your Income

- Have someone read aloud Genesis 1:27. ("God created humanity in God's own image, / in the divine image God created them, / male and female God created them.") What does this verse tell us about where our identity is based?

- How does Colossians 3:23 define what it means to be a "diligent" worker? ("Whatever you do, do it from the heart for the Lord and not for people.")

- How do you currently view your work? How do these verses encourage you in this area of your life?

- Does the perspective of working for the Lord rather than for people change the way you see your work? In what ways do you feel God prompting you to be more purposeful in your work?

Your Spending Plan: Income

- Does anyone have questions about how to calculate your net take-home pay?

- Does anyone have a variable monthly income, and if so, do you have questions about how to calculate your monthly net take-home pay?

- On page 41 of the workbook (Activity: Allocating New Income), you were asked to consider what you would do with your next raise or any other unexpected income. We encourage you to prayerfully make a plan now for that income, so that when it comes, you'll know exactly what to do with it. Would anyone like to share your plan for any extra income you might receive?

- If you haven't done so already, make sure you've entered your net income on your master Spending Plan. (Since in all likelihood your income hasn't changed since you did your pre-work, you can probably copy it from your What I Spend pre-work form.) Does anyone have a question about that?

> ## NET **TAKE-HOME** PAY:
>
> - The amount of the paycheck after all taxes and deductions.

Closing Activity and Prayer (5 minutes)

Congratulations! You've just completed the first section of your Spending Plan. You're off to a great start, doing the hard but necessary work to get your financial life on track.

Before we dismiss, let's take a few minutes to quietly think on the following question. Feel free to take notes or write down your thoughts and prayers as you reflect:

- Considering your work life, are there any adjustments you might want or need to make in order to be more line with the faithful way toward your work?

Action Plan for the Week

- In our next session, we will be interacting with the Money Motivation Quiz and the Money Autobiography form in the pre-work forms. If you haven't already completed these forms, try to do so before the next meeting.
- Begin or continue recording your daily expenses using the Spending Form provided.

Closing Prayer

Loving God, thank you for the opportunity to name and discredit the lies about our identity and our worth that our consumer culture so often sells us. Thank you for your Word, and the truth within it, that allows us to call out these lies for what they are and to claim our identity as those who are made in your image. Help us to see our work as a place where we can serve you and others, and give us eyes to see our work as holy, when done in your name. Be with us this week as we dive into tracking our expenses. Help us to see the areas in which we need to be more mindful with our resources, and help us to honor you in how we use those resources; in Jesus's name. Amen.

SESSION 3

Giving and Saving

Planning the Session

Session Goals

Through this session's discussion and activities, participants will be encouraged to:

- Understand what the consumer culture says about giving and saving;
- Learn about the faithful way toward giving and saving; and
- Complete the Giving and Saving sections of their Spending Plans.

Preparation

- Read and reflect on chapter 3 of the *Saving Grace Participant Workbook*.
- Read through this session outline in its entirety to familiarize yourself with the material being covered. Be prepared to adjust the session as group members interact and as questions arise. Prepare carefully, but allow space for the Holy Spirit to move in and through the group members and through you as facilitator.
- Read and reflect on the following Scriptures:
  - ◊ Ecclesiastes 5:10
  - ◊ Psalm 116:12
  - ◊ James 1:17

◊   Matthew 6:19-21; Matthew 6:33

◊   1 John 3:17

◊   Genesis 12:2-3

◊   Luke 21:1-4

◊   Proverbs 21:20

◊   Luke 12:16-21

- You may want to have a markerboard or large sheet of paper available for recording participants' ideas or for putting your own thoughts on the board for the group to see.

- Have a Bible, paper for taking notes, and a pen or pencil available for every participant.

- You will also want to have a calculator, computer, smart phone, or other device on hand for making any quick calculations.

- You will need access to a DVD player or another method for streaming videos online for the group to watch.

- This week you'll be asking participants to refer back to the Money Motivation Quiz and the Money Autobiography form they completed in pre-work. If you'd like, send an email reminder a few days prior to your meeting time, reminding participants to make sure they complete these forms before you meet.

- This session advocates that participants contribute or work up to a 10 percent tithe. You may wish to check with your senior pastor(s) to be sure the views on tithing expressed in this session are consistent with your church's views.

Beginning Your Time Together (5-10 minutes)

As participants arrive, welcome them. Open the group in prayer; then ask the icebreaker question and encourage participants to share their responses with the group.

Opening Prayer

Lord, guide us today as we dive deeper in learning more about your mind and heart for our finances. As we study giving and saving today, open our eyes to our motivations and desires and the ways in which we put our trust in things other than you; in Jesus's name. Amen.

Icebreaker

- How are you doing with tracking your expenses? What are you finding difficult, or helpful, about the process?

Video Session (30-35 minutes)

Watch video session (15-20 minutes in length).

Video Discussion

- In today's video, Mark (a former pastor and now a financial planner) points out that he came from a family that didn't handle finances well. Growing up, how did your family handle their finances? Was there an emphasis on giving and saving?

- As you've probably discovered already, working with your finances is a spiritual journey unto itself, revealing much about what you value. How does giving first and foremost (even above saving) help you put your money in perspective?

- Tom points out that there have been many studies done that conclude people are happier when they are generous. Have you found this to be true in your own life?

- In the video, Mark and Tom give several helpful, practical tips on giving and saving. What are some of your takeaways?

- Mark discusses that in our financial lives we sometimes suffer from "decision fatigue" and lose focus in our goals. Have you found this to be true in your own life? What are some ways you can reduce the amounts of decisions you have to make financially? (For example, setting up automatic drafts for giving or saving.)

- Many of us are anxious about starting a financial journey because we simply don't know how much we are spending, saving, and giving. Mark points out that much of this anxiety can be alleviated by simply getting honest about where you are in your finances. Have you felt anxious yet in this process? What do you think can help you move forward with more hope and confidence?

Study and Discussion (15 minutes)

WHAT OUR CONSUMER CULTURE SAYS ABOUT GIVING

- Give if it benefits you.
- Give if there is anything left over.
- Give out of a sense of duty.
- Give to get.

GIVING AND THE FAITHFUL WAY

- Giving is a response to God's goodness. (James 1:17)
- God is our source of security. (Matthew 6:19-21; Matthew 6:33)
- God cares about economic justice. (Luke 4:18)
- Giving is a way we can bless others and be blessed. (Genesis 12:2-3)

Note to Leader: *Based on the interests of your group and the time allowed, use as many or as few of these discussion topics and prompts as you'd like.*

Ask,

- As you've begun to consider and practice biblical principles when it comes to money, have you felt yourself feeling out-of-step with the consumer culture around you? If so, in what ways?

- In what areas do you feel most pressured or tempted to spend money, rather than give it or save it?

- Have someone read aloud Ecclesiastes 5:10 ("The money lover isn't satisfied with money; neither is the lover of wealth satisfied with income"). What does this verse tell us about looking to money or possessions for our self-worth?

- Do you tend to hoard money or spend frivolously? What do you think that behavior says about you?

The Generous Giver

- How have you seen God transform someone or something through another's generous giving?

- Have you ever felt the Lord leading you to give to someone or something that surprised you? What happened as a result?

- Ask one participant to read aloud Psalm 116:12 ("What can I give back to the Lord / for all the good things [God] has done for me?"). What does this verse say to us about why we give?

- Historically, what has been your attitude toward giving? How has that attitude shaped your giving habits?

- Do any of these cultural messages that we have listed resonate with you? If so, how?

> **GENEROUS GIVER:**
> One who gives with an obedient will, a joyful attitude, and a compassionate heart.

Note to Leader: *if you have access to a markerboard or large sheet of paper, write down the following* **bold** *statements. Read aloud (or ask participants to take turns reading aloud) the corresponding verses to the statements, and as a group. Ask participants to fill in the blanks based on what the verses say. You may have more than one answer.*

- **Giving is a response to** _____. (James 1:17)
  [*Answer: God's goodness*]

- **God is our source of** _____. (Matthew 6:19-21)
  [*Answer: security*]

- **God cares about** _____ _____. (1 John 3:17)
  [*Answer: economic justice*]

- **Giving is a way we can** _____ **others and** _____
  _____. (Genesis 12:2-3) [*Answer: bless / be blessed*]

Ask,

- Do any of these statements resonate with you? If so, which one(s) and why?

PRACTICAL TIPS ON GIVING

- The biblical benchmark for giving is 10 percent of income, which is called a tithe.
- Begin by giving something.
- Develop a long-term plan to reach the tithe.
- Consider your current financial situation and how you can grow in your giving.

WHAT IS A **TITHE**?

The Hebrew word *ma'aser*, translated as "tithe" throughout the Bible, literally means a "tenth" of something. Traditionally, a tithe is an offering to a church or other faith community that equals 10 percent of your income. The first mention of *ma'aser* occurs in Genesis 14:20, when "Abram gave Melchizedek one-tenth of everything."

- A final and very important reason for giving is that it breaks the hold money can so easily have on us. Money often equals power; but when I take money and release it by giving it away, it breaks the hold money can have over me. Have you found this to be true? In what ways?
- In the Activity: The Generous Giver (found on page 47 of the workbook), you were asked how God might be nudging you in the area of giving. Would anyone like to share what action steps you feel God is calling you to make?

Tithing

- Has a 10 percent tithe been a priority for your family, historically? What has been your attitude toward the tithe?
- When things are tight financially, it's tempting to believe that we can't give anything. Read aloud the story of the poor widow's offering in Luke 21:1-4. What does this Scripture tell us about giving?
- As you read and studied this week, how were you feeling led to grow in your giving?
- If you haven't done so already, in your master Spending Plan, enter the amount you are currently giving to your church as a tithe (this may be 10 percent of your current income; it may be higher or lower).
- Refer back the The Generous Giver activity on page 47 of the workbook. Were there ways that you felt God nudging you? Based on this, is there an amount you'd like to add in under "Other Contributions"? If so, remember to record that amount as well, if you haven't already done so.

The Wise Saver

- Historically, what has been your habit when it comes to savings?

- Have you believed the consumer culture's perspective on saving—either "if you have it, spend it" or "it's futile to save"? How do you think these messages have affected your financial habits?

- Saving and the faithful way:

  ◊ It is wise to save. (Proverbs 21:20)

  ◊ It is foolish, even sinful, to hoard. (Luke 12:16-21)

  ◊ Saving is putting money aside for appropriate goals. Hoarding is stockpiling beyond our needs or using our goals as excuses to build "bigger barns." We can avoid the "bigger barns" syndrome by understanding our tendencies and realizing when enough is enough. (Ecclesiastes 5:10 NLT)

- Read aloud the story of the rich man in Luke 12:16-21. What do you think this passage is trying to tell us about the heart of the rich man?

- Have you ever suffered from the "bigger barns" syndrome? What happened?

- So, if it's wise to save but foolish and sinful to hoard, how can we tell when saving has crossed the line into hoarding?
  (*Answer: Proverbs 21:20 and the story in Luke 12 both teach that it is wise to save for the unexpected but it's foolish to stockpile beyond our needs. But the key is that all along the way we're prayerfully reflecting on those goals.*)

WHAT OUR CONSUMER CULTURE SAYS ABOUT **SAVING**

- If you have it, spend it, and if you don't have it, spend it anyway.
- It is futile to save.

WISE **SAVER**

One who builds, preserves, and invests with discernment.

SAVING AND THE FAITHFUL WAY

- It is wise to save. (Proverbs 21:20)
- It is foolish, even sinful, to hoard. (Luke 12:16-21)
- Saving is putting money aside for appropriate goals.
- Hoarding is stockpiling beyond our needs or using our goals as excuses to build "bigger barns."
- How can we avoid the "bigger barns" syndrome? By understanding our tendencies and realizing when enough is enough. (Ecclesiastes 5:10 NLT)

COMPOUNDING APPLIES TO BOTH SIDES OF THE FINANCIAL EQUATION: **SAVING** AND **SPENDING.**

There's a cumulative effect of a little savings over time, and there's a cumulative effect of a little bit of overspending over time (that is, debt). An in-depth explanation of the principle of the cumulative effect and some interesting examples of the impact of compound interest appear on page 135 in the Appendix of the workbook, "The Cumulative Effect of Little Things over an Extended Period."

- On pages 51–52 in the workbook (Activity: Your Money Tendency), you were asked to consider your money tendencies by completing the Money Motivation Quiz in the pre-work. What did you learn about yourself from that exercise?

- What is one way you think your money tendency impacts you? How can you begin limiting that impact? (And if you don't know how, please ask for advice!)

- What did you learn from your Money Autobiography pre-work? How do you think your past experience with money shapes your present situation or attitude?

- We know that saving wisely is a biblical trait that we should embrace, and we know it can also be beneficial to us. On pages 52–55 of the workbook, we learned about the benefits of compounding interest, and how what we save now can grow exponentially over time. Does anyone have questions about compounding interest or the [Power of Compound Interest] charts on page 53 of the workbook?

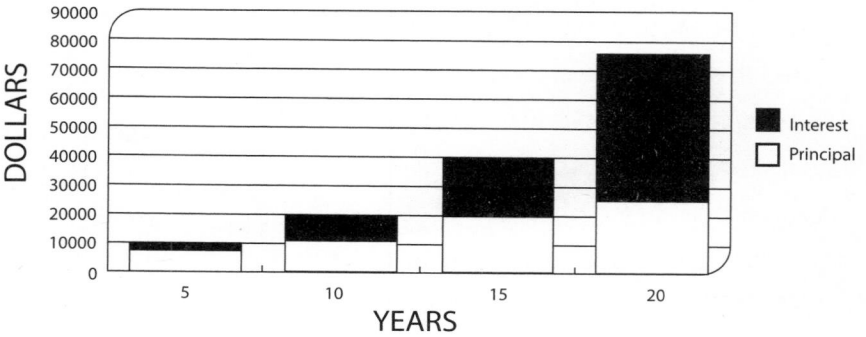

The Power of Compound Interest over 20 Years
($100/month at 10% interest)

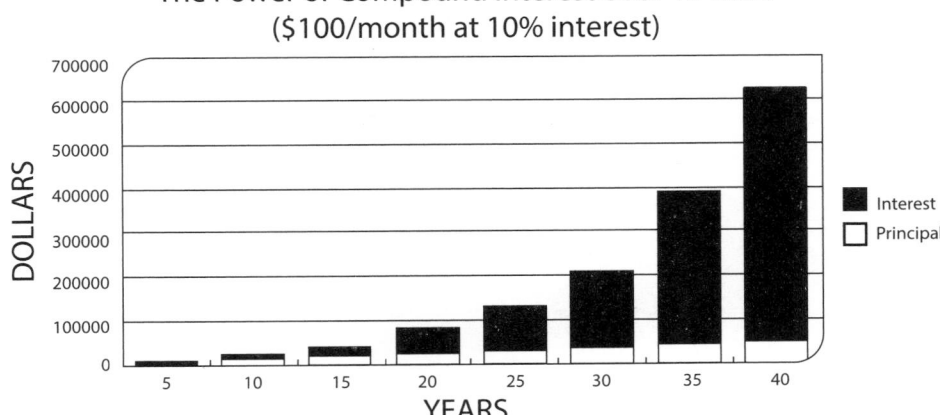

The Power of Compound Interest over 40 Years
($100/month at 10% interest)

Three Categories of Savings

- Savings fall into three categories, and should be prioritized in the following order:
  - ◊ Emergency savings,
  - ◊ Replacement savings, and
  - ◊ Long-term savings.

- What experience(s) have you had with emergency or replacement savings? For example, have you ever had need of emergency savings, and if so, were they there when you needed them? If you didn't have any reserved, how did it affect you?

- Consider your current financial situation. How are you feeling about the amount you're saving every month? If you feel it needs to be more, what are some ways you can work toward your goal?

- If you haven't done so already, add your monthly Saving goal into your Spending Plan. (If you already have an emergency savings fund, consider your goals for replacement or long-term savings. Is there an amount you can add to these funds every month? Add those amounts into your Spending Plan.)

Note to Leader: *Be sure and ask if anyone needs assistance filling out the Giving and Saving portions of their Spending Plans. You can walk them through it step by step using the information in their workbook.*

DON'T BORROW FROM YOUR RETIREMENT FUNDS, SUCH AS IRAS OR 401KS.

This is seldom a good idea. For an explanation of why borrowing from retirement funds is not wise, see the information on pages 138–139 in the Appendix of the workbook.

- How are you feeling at this point in the process of developing your Spending Goal?

Closing Activity and Prayer (5 minutes)

You have now filled out two more sections of your Spending Plan. Great job! Keep going—every step along the way matters.

- What new insights did you gain from this week's lesson on giving and what impact might they have on your finances going forward?

- What aspect of saving is most difficult for you and what action steps might you take to make savings easier?

- In which area do you feel the Lord nudging and encouraging you? What action steps might you need to take?

Action Plan for the Week

- In our next session, we will be interacting with the What I Own / What I Owe worksheet in the pre-work. If you haven't already completed this worksheet, try to do so before the next meeting.
- Continue to record your expenses this week.

Closing Prayer

Generous God, thank you for showing us how we can live generous and abundant lives by being mindful and prayerful about how you want us to give and to save. Help us to give with grateful hearts, in gratitude for what you have so freely given us. Guide us as we save so that we seek not to hoard our resources but to be wise and responsible in the process. Break the hold that money so often has on our hearts, Lord, so that we may be open and available to you; in Jesus's name. Amen.

Understanding and Eliminating Debt

Planning the Session

Session Goals

Through this session's discussion and activities, participants will be encouraged to:

- Understand the pull of the consumer culture in regard to debt;
- Explore the faithful way toward dealing with debt;
- Learn how to handle the current debt they have and avoid incurring new debt; and
- Complete the Debt section of their Spending Plans.

Preparation

- Read and reflect on chapter 4 of *Saving Grace Participant Workbook*.
- Read through this session outline in its entirety to familiarize yourself with the material being covered. Be prepared to adjust the session as group members interact and as questions arise. Prepare carefully, but allow space for the Holy Spirit to move in and through the group members and through you as facilitator.
- Read and reflect on the following Scriptures:
  - ◊ Romans 13:8
  - ◊ Matthew 5:25-34
  - ◊ Psalm 37:21a

◊   Proverbs 22:7b

◊   James 4:14; Luke 12:30-31

◊   Galatians 5:22-24

◊   Luke 12:15

◊   Deuteronomy 23:19

- You may want to have a markerboard or large sheet of paper available for recording participants' ideas or for putting your own thoughts on the board for the group to see.

- Have a Bible, paper for taking notes, and a pen or pencil available for every participant.

- You will also want to have a calculator, computer, smart phone, or other device on hand for making any quick calculations.

- You will need access to a DVD player or another method for streaming videos online for the group to watch.

- This week you'll be asking participants to refer back to the What I Own / What I Owe worksheet they completed in pre-work. If you'd like, send an email reminder a few days prior to your meeting time, reminding participants to make sure they complete this form before you meet.

Beginning Your Time Together (5-10 minutes)

As participants arrive, welcome them. Open the group in prayer; then ask the following icebreaker question and encourage participants to share their responses with the group.

Opening Prayer

Lord, we praise you for your faithfulness, even as we are often scattered and unfocused in our devotion to you. Be present in our hearts and minds today as we discuss one of the more stressful areas of our financial lives. Help us to continually put our hope in you, as we seek to know your mind and heart better; in Jesus's name. Amen.

Icebreaker

- What are you discovering as a result of tracking your expenses? Do you see any patterns or areas of your spending that seem to need attention?

Video Session (30-35 minutes)

Watch video session (15-20 minutes in length).

Video Discussion

- How do Anna and Jack describe the relationship between debt and spiritual peace? How do you think your debt has affected your spiritual life, or your discipleship journey?

- Jack points out that today's debt industry sells the idea that we can have what we want, when we want it. How have you seen advertisers, banks, media, and others pushing debt in a way that doesn't seem so bad? What are some of the tactics you've seen used?

- As this chapter points out, there are some instances of "OK debt." How does Jack point out that this type of debt can actually help you move forward in your financial goals?

- What has been your experience with student debt (yours or someone else's)? Under what circumstances should this be considered an "OK debt"?

- If debt is causing you anxiety, Jack points out that you should first be honest about your debt and make a plan to get rid of it, and then you should engage your spouse or family or community to walk with you in your goal to debt repayment. He says realizing you're not alone in the process can help you stay on track. Have you felt alone in your debt? How might you engage your family or community in walking with you through this process?

Study and Discussion (15 minutes)

Note to Leader: *Based on the interests of your group and the time allowed, use as many or as few of these discussion topics and prompts as you'd like.*

Ask,

- How have you seen debt affect someone's life? Has it ever affected your life in a significant way?

- Have a participant look up and read aloud Romans 13:8 ("Don't be in debt to anyone, except for the obligation to love each other. Whoever loves another person has fulfilled the law"). In what ways could debt affect our ability to show love to one another?

- John Wesley believed that anyone who had enough to eat and clothes to wear could be considered rich. But when debt enters the picture, he wrote, even when "a person may have more than necessaries and conveniences…[that person] is not a rich man, how much money soever he has in his hands."[1] What do you think Wesley meant?

- Debt forces us to consider how our present spending behaviors have and will impact our future. When you spend, how often are you thinking about the future impact of that money?

- Ask a participant to read aloud Matthew 5:25-34, and then discuss: Do you feel it's possible to not worry about your everyday needs? What do you think Jesus meant from this teaching?

IS **DEBT** EVER OK?

"OK" debt has two characteristics:

1. It is incurred on something that has the strong potential to increase in value, such as a home (not a depreciating or consumptive item, such as clothing or electronics).

2. It can be repaid under today's circumstances—not hoped-for circumstances in the future.

Note to Leader: *For many of us, it seems unrealistic to "not worry" about feeding our families, keeping our houses, and so on. So this passage can feel very pie-in-the-sky to many. Jesus is not asking us to be irresponsible with our needs, but instead to look to God for guidance and trust that the Lord has our best in mind. The question then becomes, where is my focus? Is it constantly on my needs and circumstances, or am I* *trying to keep my eyes on the Lord and follow where God leads? This speaks again to that "bigger barns" syndrome we talked about last session—that hoarding or stockpiling helps us feel that we are in control of the future, rather than trusting in God for provision.*

The Cautious Debtor

- What reaction do you have to the cultural myth that debt is expected and unavoidable?

- On page 61 of the workbook, the authors point out two characteristics of "OK" debt. What debt do you have that meet these criteria?

CAUTIOUS DEBTOR

One who avoids entering into debt, is careful and strategic when incurring debt, and always repays debt.

WHAT OUR CONSUMER CULTURE SAYS ABOUT DEBT

Debt is expected and unavoidable.

Note to Leader: *If you feel your group could benefit from a discussion of the power of compound interest on debt, please take a moment now to walk through that graphic (found on page 63 of the workbook). Ask, What is your reaction to this graph? Do you have any questions about it? Have you ever experienced being on the negative side of compounding debt?*

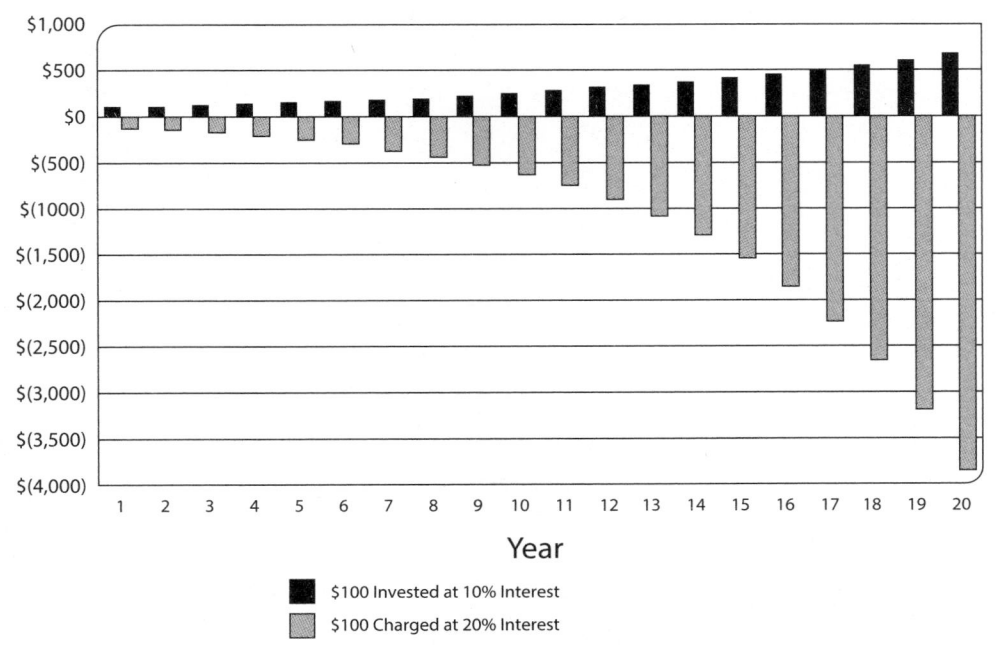

The Power of Compound Interest

Legend:
- $100 Invested at 10% Interest
- $100 Charged at 20% Interest

Note to Leader: *Assign various participants the following verses to look up in their Bibles. As you read through each point below, have participants read their corresponding assigned verses aloud.*

In this session we examine both the economic dangers of debt and the spiritual dangers of debt. The faithful way asks us to avoid debt for our own protection. Scripture encourages us to:

- Scripture encourages us to repay debt. (Psalm 37:21a))
- Debt presumes on the future, and erodes our trust in God to show love and provision to us. (James 4:14; Luke 12:30-31)
- Discipline and contentment are better values than immediate gratification. (Galatians 5:22-24)
- Envy and greed can drive us into debt. (Luke 12:15)
- Debt hurts society by preying on the vulnerable. (Deuteronomy 23:19)

- Which of these scriptural insights on debt strikes you the most? How does it change your attitude on your current debt, or how you view incurring debt in the future?
- The principles of repaying and avoiding debt might not be new to you, but have you ever thought about how incurring debt might also deny God the opportunity to provide for you? What has been your attitude toward God's provision in your life? Has it affected your view or practices regarding debt?

Breaking Down Debt

- It is helpful to understand that there are primarily five kinds of debt:
  1. Home mortgage
  2. Auto
  3. Education
  4. Business
  5. Consumer (credit cards) – the main focus of this chapter

- Do you follow the rules for using credit cards (shown on pages 67–68 of the workbook)? If so, which one have you found helpful?

- Is there a rule you need to start following in regard to your credit card usage?

- Do you agree that spending with a credit card is psychologically different than using cash? Are there examples from your own experience?

- On page 68 in the workbook, in the Activity: Your Credit Cards, you were asked to write down one action step you want to take regarding your credit or debit card(s). What is one step you plan to implement after going through this section?

- Which of the tips for using credit and debit cards (found on pages 67–68 of the workbook) did you find helpful? Does anyone have any other tips to share that he or she has learned over the years?

Paying Down Debt

- On page 70 of the workbook, you will find steps for accelerating your debt repayment:

  ◊ Incur no new debt!

  ◊ List all your debts in order from smallest to largest.

  ◊ Pay off your smallest debt first.

  ◊ As a debt is repaid, roll the amount you were paying to the next largest debt.

  ◊ Continue that strategy until all debts are paid.

Note to Leader: *If members need more guidance on creating a debt repayment plan, encourage them to study "Establishing a Debt Repayment Plan" on page 141 in the Appendix of the workbook.*

KEY QUESTION

Are you committed enough to freeing yourself from debt to find a little over three dollars a day somewhere in your expenditures that could go to debt repayment?

PROCESS FOR ACCELERATING DEBT REPAYMENT

1. Incur no new debt!
2. List all your debts in order from smallest to largest.
3. Pay off your smallest debt first.
4. As a debt is repaid, add the amount you were paying to the next largest debt.
5. Continue that strategy until all debts are paid.

For more guidance on creating a debt repayment plan, see "Establishing a Debt Repayment Plan" on page 141 in the Appendix of the workbook.

- Which of these steps for accelerating your debt payment is most challenging for you? How do you feel about listing all of your debts? Is that discouraging for you, or motivating? How are you feeling at this point in the process?

- Consider the Credit Card Debt and Repayment Example graphic on page 68 of the workbook (shown below). In this example, the authors show how adding $100 a month to your payment can help accelerate your debt repayment significantly. Breaking it down, that means you would need to find $3 per day to save in order to have the $100 for the month. In what areas could you potentially save $3 per day to put toward debt repayment?

You owe $7,200 @ 18%		
Minimum Payment = 3% of the balance or $10—whichever is greater		
You Pay	Total Paid	Time
$ Minimum/month	$14,277	20 yrs. 11 mos.
$216/month	$10,150	47 mos.
$216+100/month	$8,848	28 mos.

- Do you have questions about the Sample Debt Reduction Plan that appears on page 71 of the workbook (also shown on the following page)? What questions do you have about this process for paying down debt?

DEBT REPAYMENT IS A GREAT INVESTMENT!

- Immediate
- Tax Free
- Guaranteed
- High rate of return

Note to Leader: *Point out that participants can find a blank Debt Reduction Plan in their Appendix on page 163. Also, electronic versions of this form as well as other forms and worksheets can be found at abingdonpress .com/savinggrace. Some of the available forms will do the calculations for the participants.*

- Have you filled in the Debt section of your Spending Plan? (If you haven't done so already, use your pre-work information from the What I Own / What I Owe worksheet, list each of your debts and fill in the monthly minimum payments on your Spending Plan form.)

SAMPLE DEBT REDUCTION PLAN

Item	Amount Owed	Interest	Minimum Monthly Payment	Additional Payment $ 150	Payment Plan and Pay-off Dates				
					3 Months	6 Months	15 Months	22 Months	26 Months
Target	$372	18.0	$15	$165	paid!				
Doctor	$550	0	$20	$20	$185	paid!			
Visa	$1980	19.0	$40	$40	$40	$225	paid!		
MasterCard	$2369	16.9	$50	$50	$50	$50	$275	paid!	
Auto	$7200	6.9	$259	$259	$259	$259	$259	$534	paid!
Total	$12,471		$384	$534	$534	$534	$534	$534	0

- The first and second columns list to whom the debt is owed and the amount owed. Debts are listed in the order of lowest to highest amount.
- The third and fourth columns list the interest rate and the minimum monthly payment for each debt.
- The fifth column indicates the amount of additional payment above the minimum that can be made and adds that amount to the minimum payment for the first (smallest) debt listed.
- The remaining columns show how, as each debt is paid, the payment for it is rolled down to the next debt. Pay-off dates can be calculated in advance or simply recorded as they are achieved.

> **DEBT IS OFTEN THE SYMPTOM, NOT THE PROBLEM**
> - Discover and eliminate the root of the issue.
> - Limit your exposure to temptation.
> - Give up on one-upping your neighbors.

- Did you set a tentative goal for how much additional payment you plan to make each month? Be sure and apply this additional payment to the smallest debt on your Spending Plan.
- Just to reiterate: It is vital that you incur no new debt in this process. It will take discipline to do it, but you won't make progress if you are continuing to incur new debt as the old is being paid. How can we be accountable to each other during this difficult process?

The Benefits of Debt Repayment

- Have you ever thought about the "law of exposure" in relation to your spending? The law of exposure" says that the things we are exposed to are the things we think about, which then become the things we act upon. How can you limit your exposure to those things that tempt and pull you into more debt?
- As you worked through this session, did you discover any root issues behind your debt? If so, what is a next step you can take to address that issue?

Closing Activity and Prayer (5 minutes)

- As we wrap up, would anyone like to share any new insights about consumer debt you learned from this session?
- Dealing with our debt is not always easy. When we are tempted to overspend or break our no-new-debt rule, it will be helpful to have some reminders in place to help us keep our goals in sight. What reminders can you put in place to help you stay on track? Is there anything the group can do to help?

Action Plan for the Week

- This week, try not to use your credit card and note how that feels.

- Continue recording your daily expenses using the Spending Form provided.

- In our next session, we will be interacting with "What I Spend" from your pre-work worksheets. If you haven't already completed this worksheet, try to do so before the next meeting.

- Use the records you've been keeping to review the items in the Household/Personal category of your "What I Spend" pre-work sheet. We will talk more in the next session about how to reduce these expenses, but do any areas stand out to you as perhaps being too high?

Closing Prayer

God, thank you for continually revealing yourself to us throughout this process of aligning our finances with the life you have called us to live. We thank you for your kindness and gentleness as we work through these sensitive areas of our lives, and we praise you for your wisdom and grace to guide us. As we go about our days, help us to remember how you love us and care for us, and help us to live in that knowledge; in Jesus's name. Amen.

Spending

Planning the Session

Session Goals

Through this session's discussion and activities, participants will be encouraged to:

- Consider what it means to spend mindfully and to be a prudent spender;
- Learn more about the faithful way as it relates to spending; and
- Complete the remaining sections of their Spending Plans.

Preparation

- Read and reflect on chapter 5 of *Saving Grace Participant Workbook*.
- Read through this session outline in its entirety to familiarize yourself with the material being covered. Be prepared to adjust the session as group members interact and as questions arise. Prepare carefully, but allow space for the Holy Spirit to move in and through the group members and through you as facilitator.
- Read and reflect on the following Scriptures:
  - ◊ Deuteronomy 5:7-9; James 5:2-3
  - ◊ Luke 12:15
  - ◊ 1 Timothy 6:17-19
  - ◊ Philippians 4:12-13

- You may want to have a markerboard or large sheet of paper available for recording participants' ideas or for putting your own thoughts on the board for the group to see.

- Have a Bible, paper for taking notes, and a pen or pencil available for every participant.

- You will also want to have a calculator, computer, smart phone, or other device on hand for making any quick calculations.

- You will need access to a DVD player or another method for streaming videos online for the group to watch.

- This week you'll be asking participants to refer back to the "What I Spend" worksheet they completed in pre-work. If you'd like, send an email reminder a few days prior to your meeting time, reminding participants to make sure they complete this form before you meet.

Beginning Your Time Together (5-10 minutes)

As participants arrive, welcome them. Open the group in prayer; then ask the following icebreaker question and encourage participants to share their responses with the group.

Opening Prayer

Loving God, thank you for the opportunity to meet again today. Thank you for continually showing us that we can be diligent and faithful to you in our finances because you are faithful to us, and we can do all things in your name; in Jesus's name. Amen.

Icebreaker

- What was your experience in trying to not use credit cards this past week?

Video Session (30-35 minutes)

Watch video session (15-20 minutes in length).

Video Discussion

- Jodi says that although she was well educated in financial matters, she only experienced true financial transformation in her life when she began to learn and embrace what Scripture teaches about money. In what ways have you found this to be true in your own life?

- Tom says he was struck by the term "spending mindfulness" used in this chapter. After watching the video, how would you define it?

- Have you ever felt the draw of "retail therapy"? In what cases are you drawn to spending in that way, and how do you feel after doing so?

- Jodi says that when she realized her spending wasn't mindful, she began to curb those impulses and change her mindset by giving more instead of spending more, and that allowed her and her family to experience freedom. In what ways do you sense the Lord is asking you to curb your spending? Are you feeling led to increase your giving in some way?

- Tom asked Jodi to fill in the blank on the statement, "As I reordered and reprioritized my spending habits, I experienced more _____." Jodi's answer was "joy." How would you fill in the blank on this statement, based on what you've been learning in this study thus far?

Study and Discussion (15 minutes)

Note to Leader: *Based on the interests of your group and the time allowed, use as many or as few of these discussion topics and prompts as you'd like.*

- Wesley's questions, paraphrased below, went right back to the beliefs about money that we have discussed so far:

  1. Am I acting as a steward of God's resources?

  2. Am I living out of God's intentions as revealed in the Scripture?

  3. Can I offer up my actions with money as a sacrifice to God through Jesus Christ?, and

4. Is this expense the kind of action that lays up a reward at the resurrection?[1]

WHAT OUR CONSUMER CULTURE SAYS ABOUT SPENDING

- Things bring happiness.
- Possessions define who we are.
- The more we have, the more we should spend.
- Spending is a competition.

PRUDENT SPENDER

One who enjoys the fruits of his or her labor yet guards against materialism.

- Think back to the last purchase you made (whether large or small) and consider that purchase through the lens of Wesley's questions. How do you see that purchase now? (It's okay if you see it in a faithful light!)

- The pull of the consumer culture says:

  ◊ Things bring happiness.

  ◊ Your possessions define who you are.

  ◊ The more we have, the more we should spend.

  ◊ Spending is a competition.

- These statements are not entirely new to us since they are some of the myths and messages we've discussed throughout the course, but they all tend to converge on us in the area of spending. Which of these myths resonates most with you?

- Have any of these myths ever gotten you (or someone you know) into trouble?

- How do these myths play into the "bigger barns" syndrome that we discussed in session 3?

Spending and the Faithful Way

Note to Leader: *Ask five participants to look up one of the following verses each, and ask that person to read her or his verse out loud after you read aloud the corresponding statement. Then discuss the question that follows.*

1. Beware of idols. (Deuteronomy 5:7-9; James 5:2-3)

   ◊ What "spending idols" do you suspect have some control in your life?

2. Guard against greed. (Luke 12:15)

◊ In which areas do you sense you could exercise more moderation in your spending?

3. When we practice moderation and learn contentment, we are free to be generous and a blessing to others. (1 Timothy 6:17-19)

◊ What is one way you have shared your money, possessions, or even time with someone else who needed it?
What did that experience show you?

4. Contentment with and gratitude for what we have is the antidote to greed and envy (Philippians 4:12-13)

◊ How do you respond to the apostle Paul's words in Philippians 4:12-13?

Claiming Your Ground in Spending

- Because "When is enough, enough?" is such a key question, and because we're not often challenged to consider it, on page 81 of the workbook, in the Activity: Claiming Your Ground, you were challenged to think a little more about this concept of "enough is enough" when it comes to your spending. What is one way you plan to "claim your ground" in your lifestyle?

Categories of Spending: Housing

Note to Leader: *If you don't already know, start by asking the participants if they already own homes. If all members in your group are homeowners, you may want to skip over the discussion about buying a home versus renting. If you do have*

SPENDING AND THE FAITHFUL WAY

- Beware of idols (Deuteronomy 5:7-9; James 5:2-3).
- Guard against greed (Luke 12:15).
- When we practice moderation and learn contentment, we are free to be generous and a blessing to others (1 Timothy 6:17-19).
- Contentment with and gratitude for what we have is the antidote to greed and envy (Philippians 4:12-13).

KEY QUESTION

Are you willing to "claim your ground" in your spending lifestyle?

CLAIMING YOUR GROUND

- Claiming your ground means you are willing to declare, "Enough is enough!"
- When you claim your ground, you distinguish between your true needs and your wants (what the consumer culture says you need).

participants who are renting or considering buying a home, you will want to discuss the pros and cons of home ownership with them.

- What are the benefits of renting versus buying a home? What position should you be in before you consider buying a home? (**Hint for Leader:** *Do you have a 20 percent down payment? Are you planning to move in two to three years?*)

- It is recommended that you consider basing what you can afford on one income rather than two, so that if something happens to one income, you can still live within your means on the other. Have you heard this suggestion before? Does it seem doable to you? What would be the benefit of sacrificing a bit to make that happen?

- Do you know how to do your own basic repairs and maintenance on your home? If not, what is one new skill you could learn this month?

- Given the suggestions on page 83 of the workbook, what are some ways you might be able to cut your utility bills? Does anyone have suggestions for what has worked for you?

- Have you filled in the Housing section of your Spending Plan? (If you haven't done so already, use your pre-work information from the "What I Spend" worksheet for what you currently spend for housing. The percentage guidelines on the Spending Plan form can also help guide you. These percentages represent a suggested guideline for what percentage of your income should go into these categories.)

- Don't forget the lines for Maintenance/Repairs and all Utilities. Does anyone have questions about this?

Categories of Spending: Auto/Transportation

- The authors say the least expensive car you can drive is the one you already own. What do you think about this statement? Does it challenge your previously held notions?

- When might this become untrue? (*Answer: when the cost of repairs exceeds the value of the car.*)

- On page 85 of the workbook (shown below), there is a graphic that tells you how to pay cash for your next car. Has anyone ever done this? Do you have questions about how you can make that happen?

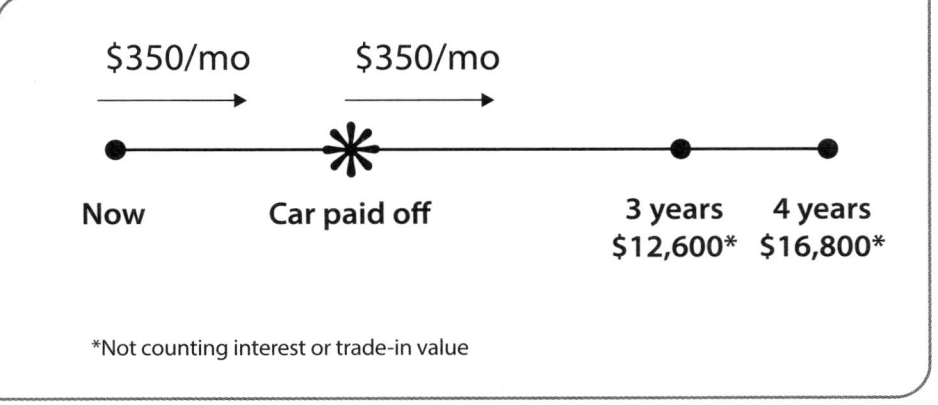

$350/mo $350/mo

Now   **Car paid off**   **3 years**   **4 years**
                                           $12,600*   **$16,800***

*Not counting interest or trade-in value

- Have you ever bought a new car, or leased a car? How do you think it affected you financially?

- Have you filled in the Auto/Transportation section of your Spending Plan? (If you haven't done so already, use your pre-work information from the "What I Spend" worksheet to fill in what you currently spend in this category. If you didn't complete the pre-work, use your best estimate of expenses. The percentage guidelines on the Spending Plan form can help you.)

- Consider any ways you can reduce these expenses. Write down at least one action step you plan to take. Set goals for these categories, and fill in those new amounts on your Spending Plan form.

Categories of Spending: Insurance

- Does anyone have questions about insurance—where to find it, what kind of coverage you need, and so forth? Can anyone offer suggestions or tips they have learned for saving money in this area?

Note to Leader: *Depending on the age of the members in your group, in addition to life insurance, you may want to encourage them to consider disability insurance and long-term care insurance. As we grow older, health problems requiring a nursing home or in-home care can create major financial problems. There are lots of pros* *and cons to long-term care insurance but as you enter your fifties, it may be wise to investigate this type of insurance.*

- Have you filled in the Insurance section of your Spending Plan? (If you haven't done so already, use your pre-work information from the "What I Spend" worksheet to fill in what you currently spend in this category. If you didn't complete the pre-work, use your best estimate of expenses. The percentage guidelines on the Spending Plan form can help you.)

- What is one way you can possibly reduce these expenses? Set goals for these categories, and fill in those amounts on your Spending Plan form.

Categories of Spending: Household/Personal, Entertainment, and Professional Services

- In your Spending Plan, have you entered an amount that you'd like to allocate to the Miscellaneous Small Cash Expenditures category? If not, do so now. (This is for small items like newspapers or coffees and other beverages/snacks you might pick up throughout the day.

- Have you filled in the Household/Personal section of your Spending Plan? (If you haven't done so already, use your pre-work information from the "What I Spend" worksheet to fill in what you currently spend in this category.)

- Have you filled in the Entertainment section of your Spending Plan? (If you haven't done so already, use your pre-work information from the "What I Spend" worksheet to fill in what you currently spend in this category.)

- Have you filled in the Professional section of your Spending Plan? (If you haven't done so already, use your pre-work information from the "What I Spend" worksheet to fill in what you currently spend in this category.)

Spending Summary

- Where do you see potential for reducing expenses in these categories of your Spending Plan?

- Which tips given in the workbook do you find helpful in reducing expenses? Can you share with the group some helpful hints you've learned? What has worked for you in the past?

- What goals would you like to set for reducing expenses in these categories? Be sure to enter those amounts on your Spending Plan form.

- Are there any categories of the Spending Plan you haven't filled out yet? If not, do so now.

- Have you totaled all your expenses and filled in the box in the lower right corner of your Spending Plan form?

Note to Leader: *Stress that, at this time, participants shouldn't be concerned about whether the income and expenses balance. We will address this in the next session.*

Closing Activity and Prayer (5 minutes)

Note to Leader: *Upon completion of the first draft of their Spending Plan, some of your group will probably discover that their expenses exceed their income—even though they have made what they consider to be significant changes for the good throughout the course. Reassure them that this is not uncommon and that the next session will speak to this situation.*

Congratulations! You've just completed the first draft of your Spending Plan. This is a big accomplishment!

- How are you feeling at this point in the process? What is the Lord showing you or teaching you during this time?

- What is the best idea you got from reading the cost-saving tips in your workbook?

Action Plan for the Week

- Complete any remaining part of your Spending Plan that you've been unable to until now.

Closing Prayer

Dear Lord, as we leave here and go about our week, remind us how much you love us and how rich we are in you. Help us to stick to our goals and to control any mindless spending. Remind us that mindful spending leads us to freedom and helps us to accomplish the purposes you have for us on this earth. Show us how to be your hands and feet to the world around us, and guide us in using our resources as we seek your will for our lives; in Jesus's name. Amen.

Adjusting the Spending Plan

Planning the Session

Session Goals

Through this session's discussion and activities, participants will be encouraged to:

- Bring their income and expenses into balance;
- Learn biblical principles for prioritizing using money;
- Move forward with their record-keeping system; and
- Find solutions for dealing with implementation issues in their Spending Plan.

Preparation

- Read and reflect on chapter 6 of *Saving Grace Participant Workbook*.
- Read through this session outline in its entirety to familiarize yourself with the material being covered. Be prepared to adjust the session as group members interact and as questions arise. Prepare carefully, but allow space for the Holy Spirit to move in and through the group members and through you as facilitator.
- Read and reflect on the following Scriptures:
  - ◊ Luke 12:22-28
  - ◊ Romans 7:15
  - ◊ Malachi 3:10

- You may want to have a markerboard or large sheet of paper available for recording participants' ideas or for putting your own thoughts on the board for the group to see.

- Have a Bible, paper for taking notes, and a pen or pencil available for every participant.

- You will also want to have a calculator, computer, smart phone, or other device on hand for making any quick calculations.

- You will need access to a DVD player or another method for streaming videos online for the group to watch.

- This week your group members will be asked to make a commitment to stick to their Spending Plan. Plan to somehow celebrate what they have accomplished thus far, and encourage them to keep going! You may want to provide refreshments or set up a potluck or decorate your space to make this a special meeting.

- Consider scheduling a follow-up meeting in four to six weeks for members to share how they are doing in implementing their Spending Plan and recording their expenses. Make it a time of celebration, encouragement, and prayer for one another. (If you're unable to gather again at that time, plan to follow up with each member individually to check on his or her progress.

Beginning Your Time Together (5-10 minutes)

As participants arrive, welcome them. Open the group in prayer; then ask the following icebreaker question and encourage participants to share their responses with the group.

Opening Prayer

Lord, once again we come to you and thank you for this opportunity to meet together and to support and encourage one another as we take control of the resources you have so graciously given us. Through this process, we pray that we would know you better and know ourselves better, God, so that we can wholeheartedly live into your plan for our lives; in Jesus's name. Amen.

Icebreaker

- What cost-saving practices were you able to put into effect this past week?

- How are you feeling thus far about following your plan?

Video Session (30-35 minutes)

Watch video session (15-20 minutes in length).

Video Discussion

- In this session Tom and Twanda talk about how faithfully managing our money helps us gain financial freedom. Have you experienced freedom in any areas since beginning this study?

- Twanda points out that it's important to understand your own history and financial habits and mindsets as you continue on the road to financial freedom. How have some of the forms included in this study—such as the Money Autobiography—helped you come to grips with your own financial philosophy?

- Accountability is very important in this process. Tom talks about an instance in which his wife encouraged him in staying on track with their spending goals. Who is your "accountability partner" in your Spending Plan? (If you're single or managing this process on your own, Tom and Twanda say that a Spending Plan can function as that accountability partner you need to stay on track.)

- One of the most important aspects of successfully using your Spending Plan is to find out which system of record keeping works for you. Twanda also points out that the system that works for you may not be the same system that works for someone else and that you might have to try out all the systems before finding your perfect one. Which one has been working for you so far?

- Twanda describes how, in her younger life, she felt held down by her debt, and her brother encouraged her to use the "snowball effect" in paying it off. Have you had experience with this strategy in your own life (or seen it work for someone else)?

Study and Discussion (15 minutes)

Note to the leader: *Based on the interests of your group and the time allowed, use as many or as few of these discussion topics and prompts as you'd like.*

PRIORITIZING MONEY

- Consumer culture says spend on lifestyle first, and then give and save.
- The faithful way is to give first, then save, then consider lifestyle spending.

TRANSITIONING OUT OF DEBT

- Give something.
- Save something.
- Aim for maximum repayment of debt.
- Minimize lifestyle spending to maximize funds available for debt repayment.

Ask,

- How would you describe your current state of mind when it comes to your finances—aware and attentive or worried?
- Ask someone to read aloud Luke 12:24 and Luke 12:27-28. How do these verses encourage you in the way that the Lord sees you and takes care of you?
- When was a time in your life that you recognized God was being generous to you?
- Now that you are able to see your income in comparison to your total expenses, you will see one of three possible scenarios:
  1. Your income equals your expenses. (This is a balanced plan.)
  2. Your income exceeds your expenses.
  3. Your expenses exceed your income.

Note to Leader: *If you feel it's appropriate to ask participants where they are right now, you can do so but don't push anyone to share. You might want to share when you've been in one of these situations and how you felt (especially if you were in scenario #3). Encourage participants not to be discouraged, but to know there is a way out and you'll help them get this under control.*

Prioritizing the Four Uses of Money

- Have you ever found yourself in a situation that sent you out of control financially? How did affect you, both economically and spiritually?

- What do you typically choose to spend your money on first—lifestyle or giving/saving?

- So let's look at a different order for the things we can do with money, which begins with God's intentions in mind. This order is:
  - ◊ giving,
  - ◊ saving,
  - ◊ *then* lifestyle.

- If you are already in debt and working to transition out of debt, here's how to move forward. (**Leader:** *If possible, write these phrases on a markerboard or large sheet of paper.*)
  - ◊ Give *something.*
  - ◊ Save *something.*
  - ◊ Live a *Spartan* lifestyle.

- During this transitional phase, do you need to adjust what you are currently **giving**? If you're finding it hard to give, decide to just give something. (Adjust the amount you've decided to give on your Spending Plan.)

- Do you need to adjust what you are currently **saving**? If you're finding it hard to save, decide to just save *something*. (Adjust the amount you've decided to save on your Spending Plan.)

- How do you feel about living a Spartan lifestyle? Where can you start today to cut back in one area of your spending in order to save or pay back debt? (Adjust that amount on your Spending Plan.)

HOW TO BRING INCOME AND EXPENSES INTO BALANCE

1. Increase income.
   But simply increasing income does not deal with the root problem of why expenses exceed income.
2. Sell assets to pay off some debt.
   This may be wise but also does not deal with the root problem.
3. Reduce expenses to live within your existing income.
   Do I have optional expenses I can eliminate?
   Do I have variable expenses I can further reduce?
   Can I eliminate any assumptions about "fixed" expenses?

How to Bring Income and Expenses into Balance

- If your Spending Plan is out of balance, we have some strategies we recommend to get things back in order. There are three main ways to do this.
  1. Increase income.
  2. Sell assets to pay off some debt.
  3. Reduce expenses to live within your existing income.
- Keeping in mind that the key to a balanced Spending Plan is to live within your income, how could one (or more) of these three options help you balance your plan?
- Did asking the questions on page 108 of your workbook about reducing your expenses help you find some areas in which you might be able to save money?
- How can we help you make adjustments to your Spending Plan?

Note to Leader: *At this point, you might want to ask what questions participants have about adjusting their plan. They should have tried to balance their plans on their own prior to the meeting, but they may still have questions or need help. Use the following to aid you in helping them make adjustments.*

Moving Forward with the Plan: Record Keeping

- There are four benefits of record keeping. Record keeping:
  1. Gives accurate data.
  2. Improves marital communication.
  3. Allows for midcourse corrections.
  4. Provides a form of accountability.

- In which of these ways do you think record keeping will help you the most?

- There are three record-keeping systems we recommend:
  1. Using the envelope system,
  2. Keeping written records, or
  3. Using an electronic platform.

- Have you already been using one of these systems? If so, what do you like or dislike about it?

- Do you have specific questions about any of the systems discussed here?

- On pages 116–117 of the workbook (Activity: Selecting Your Record-Keeping System), you were asked to select which record-keeping

Envelope System: A tangible way to designate money for various expenses

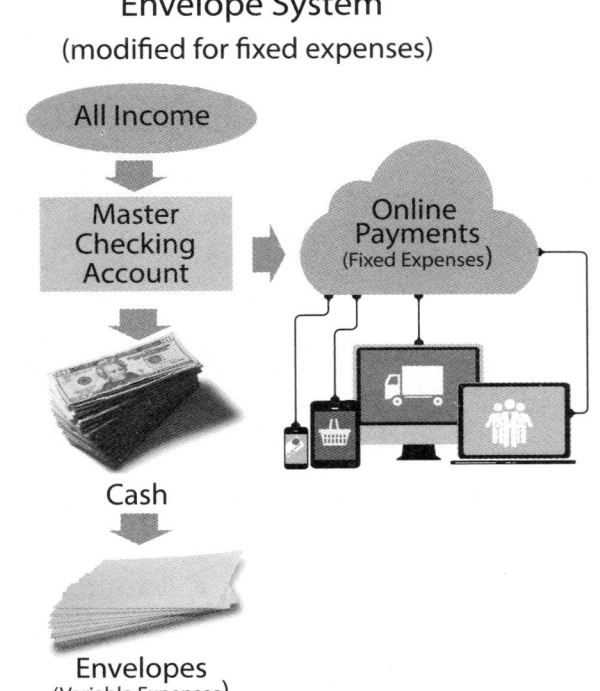

Envelope System

All Income

Master Checking Account

Cash

Envelopes

Envelope System
(modified for fixed expenses)

All Income

Master Checking Account

Online Payments
(Fixed Expenses)

Cash

Envelopes
(Variable Expenses)

If you receive more than one paycheck per month, create a plan for which expenses will be paid out of each paycheck. For a sample plan, see page 159 in the Appendix of the workbook.

If you have money accumulating in certain categories, transfer funds from those categories into a short-term savings account. Use a simple ledger to keep track of how much money in the account is in each category. For a sample ledger, see page 162 in the Appendix of the workbook.

DEALING WITH EMERGENCIES

- Keep your commitment not to incur new debt.
- Look at your Spending Plan to see where else you may be able to save money.
- Think creatively.
- Let others know of your need.

The more we become financially faithful, the closer we get to true financial well-being.

system you plan to use to implement your Spending Plan: envelope, written record, electronic, or a combination. Which did you choose, and why?

Tip: *If you plan on using the written or electronic systems, transfer the numbers from your Spending Plan form to the first lines of the blank Spending Record form on pages 167–168 of your Appendix. You can use those numbers to help you set up your electronic record-keeping system. If you plan on using the envelope system, use the Envelope Record-Keeping Worksheet, found on page 165 of the Appendix to designate your spending categories and amounts. Under the Checks/Automatic Withdrawal section, write in any expenses you plan to pay with a check or automatic withdrawal.*

Dealing with Implementation Issues and Emergencies

- On page 118 of the workbook, in the Activity: Obstacles, you were asked to identify a couple of issues you may encounter when you begin implementing your Spending Plan and record-keeping system. For your particular situation, what are some obstacles you might face?

Note to Leader: *If someone identifies an issue she or he is having, offer your own advice and/or ask if anyone else has encountered these issues and has any words of advice in that area.*

- What amount do you have allocated for emergency savings? If you don't have any amount listed, what small goal can you make for putting some money into that fund so that emergencies don't drive you deeper into debt? Where can you save a little extra money for that purpose?

MONTH: *January*

Daily Variable Expenses

	Transportation		Household						Professional Services	Entertainment		
	Gas, etc.	Maint./ Repair	Groceries	Clothes	Gifts	Household Items	Personal	Other	Going Out	Travel	Other
(1) Spending Plan	200	40	480	150	80	75	50	---	---	100	70	40
	64	21	186	89	17	14	16	25	---	22	70	22 (sitter)
	42	22	46	17	55	22	18			46		
	38	20	20	50		9				19		
	58		172			31						
			18									
			8									
			20									
(2) Total	202	21	446	185	72	76	34	25	---	87	70	22
(3) (Over)/Under	(2)	19	34	(35)	8	(1)	16	(25)	---	13	---	18
(4) Last Mo. YTD												
(5) This Mo. YTD												

1 2 3 4 5 6 7 8 9 10 11 12 13 14 15 16 17 18 19 20 21 22 23 24 25 26 27 28 29 30 31

- Use this page to record expenses that tend to be daily, variable expenses—often the hardest to control.
- Keep receipts throughout the day and record them at the end of each day.
- Total each category at the end of the month (line 2) and compare to the Spending Plan (line 1). Subtracting line 2 from line 1 gives you an (over) or under the budget figure for that month (line 3).
- To verify that you have made each day's entry, cross out the number at the bottom of the page that corresponds to that day's date.
- Optional: If you wish to monitor your progress as you go through the year, you can keep cumulative totals in lines 4 and 5.

SPENDING RECORD EXAMPLE

MONTH: January

Monthly Regular Expenses (generally paid by check once a month)

	Giving		Savings	Debt			Housing				Auto Payments	Insurance		Misc. Cash Expenses
	Church	Other		Credit Cards	Education	Other	Mortgage/Rent	Maintenance	Utilities	Other		Auto/Home	Life/Medical	
(1) Spending Plan	280	30	155	75	50	---	970	30	180	25	350	90	40	65
	140	20	155	75	50	---	970	---	95 (elec)	44	350		40	65
	140	10	200						31 (gas)					
									79 (tel)					
(2) Total	280	30	355	75	50	---	970	---	205	44	350	---	40	65
(3) (Over)/Under	---	---	(200)	---	---	---	---	30	(25)	(19)	---	90	---	---
(4) Last Mo. YTD														
(5) This Mo. YTD														

- This page allows you to record major monthly expenses for which you typically write just one or two checks per month.
- Entries can be recorded as the checks are written (preferably) or by referring back to the check ledger at a convenient time.
- Total each category at the end of the month (line 2) and compare to the Spending Plan (line 1). Subtracting line 2 from line 1 gives you an (over) or under the budget figure for that month (line 3).
- Use the "Monthly Assessment" section to reflect on the future actions that will be helpful in staying on course.

MONTHLY ASSESSMENT

Area	(Over)/Under	Reason	Future Action
Clothes	(35)	After-Christmas Sales	No new clothes next month
Savings	(200)	Gift from Aunt Mary	N/A
Utilities	(25)	Electricity and phone	check phone plan
Insurance	90	Quarterly bill next month	N/A

Areas of Victory Feels great to be ahead on savings. Thanks, Aunt Mary! I'm really proud of how we're doing!

Areas to Watch Need to look hard at ways to save on electricity and phone bills.

Committing to the Process

- On page 120 of the workbook, in the Activity: My Vision for Becoming Financially Faithful, Financially Free, you were asked to imagine what your life might be like if you could become financially faithful and experience true financial freedom. Would anyone like to share your thoughts on what you envision?

- We encourage you to complete the Commitment Plan on page 121 of your workbook to remind you of why you wanted to do this in the first place and to refer back to it when you face obstacles in following your plan. The first statement on the Commitment Plan asks for a date by which you will begin implementing your Spending Plan and keeping records, and will do so for **the next ninety days**. If you haven't already, take a moment and fill in that date.

- The next statement asks for the name of an accountability partner. If you haven't already, take a moment to write down the name of someone who will be an encouragement and help hold you accountable to following your plan.

> ### KEEPING YOUR COMMITMENT TO THE SPENDING PLAN
>
> - Commit to using your Spending Plan and record-keeping system for at least ninety days.
> - Do not become discouraged after the first month—adjustments are normal.
> - Seek assistance, if needed.

Closing Activity and Prayer (5 minutes)

- Before we dismiss, would anyone be willing to share: What part of this course's teaching has really stuck with you?

- In what ways are you most encouraged to discover God's will for your life through your finances?

- In the Book of Malachi, God speaks to the people and asks them to bring their offerings on the assumption that they are giving in an environment of abundance. "Please test me in this, / says the LORD of heavenly forces. / See whether I do not open all the windows of the heavens for you / and empty out a blessing until there is enough" (Malachi 3:10). What if we trusted that we will see blessings as we attend to our financial life? How does this encourage you in your journey to financial freedom?

Note to Leader: *In 2020, the economic shutdown due to the COVID-19 crisis put many people into a situation of financial crisis. If there are people in your group who have been particularly affected, read or walk the group through "Saving Grace in a Time of Crisis" on pages 125–128 of the workbook.*

Closing Prayer

God of abundant life, we know that in your power you work transformations in the world and in our lives. You change us from within and make each of us a new person. Help us to claim a new way of thinking and a new way of living and to be good stewards of what you've entrusted to us. Empower us to live humbly and walk with you. We yearn to hear your words, "Well done, good and faithful servant, good and faithful trustee"; in Christ's name we pray. Amen.

Action Plan

Note to Leader: *Consider setting up a meeting in four to six weeks for members to share how they are doing in implementing their Spending Plan and recording their expenses. Make it a time of celebration, encouragement, and prayer for one another. If that is not possible, assure members that you will be following up with them during that time to check in and see how they are doing. Or ask them to set an alarm on their calendar to send you an update via email.*

About the Contributors

The Rev. **Tom Berlin** serves as Lead Pastor of Floris UMC, a multisite congregation with vital mission partnerships in Northern Virginia and around the globe. He attended Virginia Tech and Candler School of Theology and has authored several books and small group studies published by Abingdon Press.

Jack Brooks is the Executive Director of the Mid-Atlantic United Methodist Foundation. Prior to joining the Foundation, Jack was an executive in the investment and financial planning industry.

Mark G. Cooke is President/CEO of Heritage Financial, LLC, and wealth management firm in Gainesville, Virginia. He served as associate pastor in churches in West Virginia and Virginia before transitioning his career into financial services.

The Rev. **Anna Guillozet** is the senior pastor of Linworth United Methodist Church in Columbus, Ohio. She is a graduate of Ohio Northern University, holds an MDiv degree from the Methodist Theological School in Ohio, and will complete her dissertation for her DMin degree Fall 2020.

The Reverend **Cary James, Jr.,** is an elder in the Baltimore-Washington Conference of The United Methodist Church. Rev. James is currently the senior pastor of Jones Memorial United Methodist Church in Washington, D.C. He serves as coach and facilitator for the Mid-Atlantic United Methodist Foundation's Academy for Church Finance and Financial Leadership Academy.

The Rev. **Twanda Prioleau** has been a trained coach since 2013. She has used her gift of coaching and over thirty-five years of experience of working in the accounting field to coach individuals and churches. She is an ordained elder in The United Methodist Church and the pastor of Christ United Methodist Church in Baltimore City.

Following twenty years in the financial services industry working for nonprofit firms, tax, and financial planning as a CPA, the Rev. **Jodi Smith** answered a call to ministry in The United Methodist Church. She earned her MDiv at Perkins School of Theology at SMU. She served as both an associate pastor and as a senior pastor for nine years in the North Texas Annual Conference.

Forms

Included on the following pages are forms used in this study. These include the Debt Reduction Plan, Form for Tracking Short-Term Savings, Envelope Record-Keeping Worksheet, the Spending Plan, and the Spending Record.

NEED EXTRA **WORKSHEETS** OR **FORMS**?

Additional copies of the worksheets and forms in the workbook can be found in PDF format at abingdonpress.com/savinggrace. For those who may prefer an interactive form of the worksheets, the website also offers PDF versions that will perform the calculations in the exercises for you.

FORM #1: DEBT REDUCTION PLAN

Item	Amount Owed	Interest	Minimum Monthly Payment	Additional Payment $___	Payment Plan and Pay-off Dates						
Total											

- The first and second columns list to whom the debt is owed and the amount owed. Debts are listed in the order of lowest to highest amount.
- The third and fourth columns list the interest rate and the minimum monthly payment for each debt.
- The fifth column indicates the amount of additional payment above the minimum that can be made and adds that amount to the minimum payment for the first (smallest) debt listed.
- The remaining columns show how, as each debt is paid, the payment for it is rolled down to the next debt. Pay-off dates can be calculated in advance or simply recorded as they are achieved.

FORM #2: FORM FOR TRACKING SHORT-TERM SAVINGS

Month: _____

Date	Description	Total Fund Balance	Fund #1	Fund #2	Fund #3	Fund #4	Fund #5

FORM #3: ENVELOPE RECORD-KEEPING WORKSHEET

Envelope Record-Keeping Worksheet

Envelopes

The boxes below represent envelopes in which you will place cash for variable expenses each month. For each category, write in the category name (clothing, food, etc.) and the budgeted amount.

Category: _____
$ _____

Category: _____
$ _____

Category: _____
$ _____

Category: _____
$ _____

Category: _____
$ _____

Category: _____
$ _____

Category: _____
$ _____

Category: _____
$ _____

Checks/Automatic Withdrawals

Use the entries below to list the regular monthly expenses that you will pay by check or automatic withdrawal.

Category: _____
$ _____

Category: _____
$ _____

Category: _____
$ _____

Category: _____
$ _____

Category: _____
$ _____

Category: _____
$ _____

Category: _____
$ _____

Category: _____
$ _____

FORM #4: SPENDING PLAN

What I Spend

Earnings/Income Per Month	Totals
Salary #1 (net take-home)	_____
Salary #2 (net take-home)	_____
Other (less taxes)	_____
Total Monthly Income	$ _____

% Guide*

1. Giving $ _____

- Church _____
- Other Contributions _____

2. Savings   15% $ _____

- Emergency _____
- Replacement _____
- Long Term _____

3. Debt   0-10% $ _____

Credit Cards:
- Visa _____
- MasterCard _____
- Discover _____
- American Express _____
- Gas Cards _____
- Department Stores _____

Education Loans _____

Other Loans:
- Bank Loans _____
- Credit Union _____
- Family/Friends _____
- Other _____

4. Housing   25-36% $ _____

- Mortgage/Taxes/Rent _____
- Maintenance/Repairs _____

Utilities:
- Electric _____
- Gas _____
- Water _____
- Trash and Recycling _____
- Telephone/Internet _____
- TV/Streaming Services _____
- Other _____

5. Auto/Transp.   15-20% $ _____

- Car Payments/License _____
- Gas & Bus/Train/Parking _____
- Oil/Lube/Maintenance _____

*This is a percent of total monthly income. These are guidelines only and may be different for individual situations. However, there should be good rationale for a significant variance.

6. Insurance (Paid by you)   5% $ _____

- Auto _____
- Homeowners _____
- Life _____
- Medical/Dental _____
- Other _____

7. Household/Personal   15-25% $ _____

- Groceries _____
- Clothes/Dry Cleaning _____
- Gifts _____
- Household Items _____

Personal:
- Tobacco & Alcohol _____
- Cosmetics _____
- Barber/Beauty _____

Other:
- Books/Magazines/Music _____
- Allowances _____
- Personal Technology _____
- Extracurricular Activities _____
- Education _____
- Pets _____
- Miscellaneous _____

8. Entertainment   5-10% $ _____

Going Out:
- Meals _____
- Movies/Events _____
- Babysitting _____

Travel (Vacation/Trips) _____

Other:
- Fitness/Sports _____
- Hobbies _____
- Media Subscriptions _____
- Other _____

9. Prof. Services   5-15% $ _____

- Child Care _____
- Medical/Dental/Prescriptions _____

Other:
- Legal _____
- Counseling _____
- Professional Dues _____

10. Misc. Small Cash Expenditures   2-3% $ _____

Total Expenses $ _____

TOTAL MONTHLY INCOME	$ _____
LESS TOTAL EXPENSES	$ _____
INCOME OVER/(UNDER) EXPENSES	$ _____

FORM #5: SPENDING RECORD

MONTH: _____

Daily Variable Expenses

	Transportation		Household					Professional Services	Entertainment		
	Gas, etc.	Maint./ Repair	Groceries	Clothes	Gifts	Household Items	Personal	Other	Going Out	Travel	Other
(1) Spending Plan											
1											
2											
3											
4											
5											
6											
7											
8											
9											
10											
11											
12											
13											
14											
15											
16											
17											
18											
19											
20											
21											
22											
23											
24											
25											
26											
27											
28											
29											
30											
31											
(2) Total											
(3) (Over)/Under											
(4) Last Mo. YTD											
(5) This Mo. YTD											

- Use this page to record expenses that tend to be daily, variable expenses—often the hardest to control.
- Keep receipts throughout the day and record them at the end of each day.
- Total each category at the end of the month (line 2) and compare to the Spending Plan (line 1). Subtracting line 2 from line 1 gives you an (over) or under the budget figure for that month (line 3).
- To verify that you have made each day's entry, cross out the number at the bottom of the page that corresponds to that day's date.
- Optional: If you wish to monitor your progress as you go through the year, you can keep cumulative totals in lines 4 and 5.

FORM #5: SPENDING RECORD

MONTH: _____

Monthly Regular Expenses (generally paid by check once a month)

	Giving		Savings	Debt			Housing				Auto Payments	Insurance		Misc. Cash Expenses
	Church	Other		Credit Cards	Education	Other	Mortgage/Rent	Maintenance	Utilities	Other		Auto/Home	Life/Medical	
(1) Spending Plan														
(2) Total														
(3) (Over)/Under														
(4) Last Mo. YTD														
(5) This Mo. YTD														

- This page allows you to record major monthly expenses for which you typically write just one or two checks per month.
- Entries can be recorded as the checks are written (preferably) or by referring back to the check ledger at a convenient time.
- Total each category at the end of the month (line 2) and compare to the Spending Plan (line 1). Subtracting line 2 from line 1 gives you an (over) or under the budget figure for that month (line 3).
- Use the "Monthly Assessment" section to reflect on the future actions that will be helpful in staying on course.

MONTHLY ASSESSMENT

Area	(Over)/Under	Reason	Future Action

Areas of Victory _____

Areas to Watch _____

Notes

Session 4

1. John Wesley, Sermon 126, "On the Danger of Increasing Riches," 11, 2, http://wesley.nnu.edu/john-wesley/the-sermons-of-john-wesley-1872 -edition/sermon-126-on-the-danger-of-increasing-riches/. Accessed July 26, 2020.

Session 5

1. John Wesley, Sermon 50, "The Use of Money," III, 4, http://wesley.nnu.edu /john-wesley/the-sermons-of-john-wesley-1872-edition/sermon-50-the -use-of-money/. Accessed July 26, 2020.